Evil Empire

A Reckoning with Power

This issue of *Boston Review* is made possible by the generous support of the CAMERON SCHRIER FOUNDATION and an ANONYMOUS DONOR.

Editors-in-Chief Deborah Chasman & Joshua Cohen

Executive Editor Chloe Fox

Managing Editor Adam McGee

Senior Editor Matt Lord

Engagement Editor Rosie Gillies

Editorial Assistants Rosemarie Ho & Spencer Quong

Publisher Louisa Daniels Kearney

Marketing and Development Manager Dan Manchon

Finance Manager Anthony DeMusis III

Book Distributor The MIT Press, Cambridge, Massachusetts, and London, England

Magazine Distributor Disticor Magazine Distribution Services 800-668-7724, info@disticor.com

Printer Sheridan PA

Board of Advisors Derek Schrier (chairman), Archon Fung, Deborah Fung, Alexandra Robert Gordon, Richard M. Locke, Jeff Mayersohn, Jennifer Moses, Scott Nielsen, Robert Pollin, Rob Reich, Hiram Samel, Kim Malone Scott

Cover and Graphic Design Zak Jensen

Typefaces Druk and Adobe Pro Caslon

Evil Empire is *Boston Review* Forum 8 (43.4)

To become a member, visit:
bostonreview.net/membership/

For questions about donations and major gifts,
contact: Dan Manchon, dan@bostonreview.net

For questions about memberships, call 877-406-2443
or email Customer_Service@bostonreview.info.

Boston Review
PO Box 425786, Cambridge, MA 02142
617-324-1360

ISSN: 0734-2306 / ISBN: 978-1-946511-11-9

CONTENTS

Editors' Note

Deborah Chasman & Joshua Cohen

JUST OUTSIDE OF TUCSON, at the Davis–Monthan Air Force Base, more than 4,000 decommissioned military aircraft sit patiently in the dry heat. These old bombers, jets, and helicopters, arranged in neat rows and geometric formations, together form the largest aircraft "boneyard" in the world—a strange spectacle when viewed on Google Earth, as our cover image shows.

A boneyard, though perhaps not a graveyard. The climate provides near perfect storage conditions: while some aircraft will be broken down and cannibalized for scrap metal, others may be "reanimated" and returned to active use. Civilians employed by the base, for example, have converted old fighter jets into aerial target drones.

The Tucson air force base is a symbol of U.S. military power and an emblem of the life of empire—how empires are born in lethal force, follow an organizational logic, and then, just when you think they have crashed and burned, you discover that they are lying dormant, ready to strike again.

This *Boston Review* forum revolves around these ideas—the motivations for empire, its life and consequences, and its surprising resilience.

As part of a cross-disciplinary project, our contributors grapple with the economic, technological, racial, historical, and rhetorical elements of empire. Whatever their disciplinary angle, they have approached the theme with intellectual imagination and a sense of urgency.

"All history," as Maximillian Alvarez notes in his essay, "is the history of empire—a bid for control of that greatest expanse of territory, the past." Our hope is that by examining and understanding this history, we can strengthen the fight for a better future.

September 28, 2018

Chasman & Cohen

The End of the End of History

Maximillian Alvarez

AMONG THE PRIZES at stake in the endless war of politics is history itself. The battle for power is always a battle to determine who gets remembered, how they will be recalled, where and in what forms their memories will be preserved. In this battle, there is no room for neutral parties: every history and counter-history must fight and scrap and claw and spread and lodge itself in the world, lest it be forgotten or forcibly erased. All history, in this sense, is the history of empire—a bid for control of that greatest expanse of territory, the past.

The greatest act of empire, of course, is to declare the whole messy, brutal process finished, to climb to the top of the trash heap and trumpet one's reign as the culmination of all history. The greatest act of history, on the other hand, is to reveal such declarations to be always premature. Seneca's Pax Romana announced a history stilled by the glorious rise of Augustus, the "sun that never set" shone on the image of time frozen at the height of the British Empire—and the world spun madly on.

Nearly thirty years ago, American political scientist Francis Fukuyama famously called the ball game once more. In a 1989 essay, which he expanded into the 1992 book *The End of History and the Last Man*, Fukuyama prophesied that the fall of communism signaled "the end of history as such: that is, the end point of mankind's ideological evolution and the universalization of Western liberal democracy as the final form of human government."

Of course, the "end of history" didn't mean the end of military conflicts, social upheavals, or economic booms and busts. It did mean, however, that all boats were ultimately heading to the same shore; with no more serious contenders on the world stage, all things were trending toward a global order in which the marriage of market capitalism and liberal democracy would enjoy eternal dominance. Thus, in Fukuyama's view, the endless roil of intra- and international conflicts that have continually punctured our world during the past three decades has nothing to do with any world-historical battle between competing social orders. Rather, it merely represents the thrashing of those parts of the world that are still mired "in history" as they are compelled down the inevitable path to joining the "posthistorical" world.

There is a quasi-religious overtone to all of this—everything in the past has been moving toward a *telos*, a predestined end. The age of global neoliberalism, with a sort of egg wash of liberal democracy, stands as the inevitable endgame of "mankind's ideological evolution," the output that the entire Rube Goldberg machine of human history has always been grinding toward.

It is important to note, though, that it never really mattered whether this was what anyone wanted. If we move beyond all the fancy window dressing, we see that Fukuyama is describing the final stage not of collective human development, but of historical war and domination—of empire. In "The End of History?" he writes:

> The spectacular abundance of advanced liberal economies and the infinitely
> diverse consumer culture made possible by them seem to both foster and

preserve liberalism in the political sphere. I want to avoid the materialist determinism that says that liberal economics inevitably produces liberal politics, because I believe that both economics and politics presuppose an autonomous prior state of consciousness that makes them possible. But that state of consciousness that permits the growth of liberalism seems to stabilize in the way one would expect at the end of history if it is underwritten by the abundance of a modern free market economy.

With a sort of Clintonian optimism, Fukuyama regularly touts the fulfillment people will find in the neoliberal order at the "end of history." From "spectacular [material] abundance" to self-validation and equal representation, the marriage of market capitalism and Western liberal democracy will provide, plugging the deepest holes of want in our bodies and our souls. At the same time, Fukuyama is essentially describing the mechanical workings of a life-governing apparatus that will whistle and froth and steam on whether your wants are met or not.

One could argue that the greatest support for Fukuyama's argument is the fact that, *even if* the globalized marriage of market capitalism and liberal democracy does not constitute an ideal social order in regard to humanity's collective fulfillment, prosperity, peace, or happiness, it still seems to mark the decisive end to our development by way of outright domination. This is the subtext to the innocuous-sounding, jargony point that the particular "state of consciousness that permits the growth of liberalism seems to stabilize in the way one would expect at the end of history." Translation: the neoliberal order will "stabilize" its own dominance by continually incentivizing, rewarding, and securing the dominance of those who believe that it truly *is* the culmination of human development. Their faith in the "end of history" is validated by the enduring fact of neoliberalism—the world itself stands as a monument to their historical vision.

For the rest of us, neoliberalism has embedded itself so thoroughly in the organization of human life around the globe that any of our quixotic attempts to challenge its dominance will be overwhelmed, neutralized, extinguished, or absorbed. In other words, we are not necessarily born again and remade by the world order at the "end of history" to be any more convinced that this is how things were supposed to be, that this is where history was always supposed to end up. Rather, in our daily subjugation to the dominant world order, we are materially and soulfully incentivized to believe that, as the deathly adage goes, "there is no alternative."

At base, then, it is clear that Fukuyama is describing a world-historical scenario in which one people's history has permanently dominated that of all others—the end of history by fiat. Again, ours is not the first imperial age to declare itself the ultimate inheritor of the mantle of history itself. And the history we have inherited is littered with the bones of empires that inevitably crumbled, receded, and were usurped by some challenger. In the absence of a totalizing system of global control, the territorial empires of old were always susceptible to threats from beyond their own borders, always vulnerable to rot and revolt from within. What allegedly distinguishes our time from others, though, is the fact that the violent spread of market capitalism has "territorialized" nations and states around the globe, brought them into the collective fold, to the point that there *is no "outside"* anymore—no external threats to be vulnerable to. Thus, with every state on the planet being made functionally dependent on the global circuits of capitalism, every point of disruption from within will be swarmed and brought to heel under the sheer heft of the whole.

Whether or not we want history to keep moving toward something else, something better than this, the suffocating reach of market capitalism and the legion of liberal democratic outposts and extranational bodies that secure its dominance around the world leaves us wondering: Where could history possibly go from here? And where would the forces that move history even come from?

FUKUYAMA'S TAKE on the "end of history," to be fair, has been questioned for decades. And for a number of reasons: from its Eurocentrism to its unshakeable faith in the world-historical stability of a neoliberal apparatus securing and enforcing the global marriage of "free trade" and Western liberal democracy. The past decade alone would seem to pose as great a challenge as we have seen to the Fukuyaman conceit. From the 2008 global financial crash to the rise of authoritarian-minded, far-right, Trump-style "populism," the neoliberal order has shown quite a lack of, well, stability.

The very same empire that is supposed to lord over this end of history, forever and ever amen, can no longer seem to keep its story straight. Even as Donald Trump lauds himself as the very best president ever—an end-of-history sentiment if ever there was one—his presidency is nonetheless anchored to the message that the United States must be made great *again*. Something has slipped; the end of history has gone too far, and we must try to go back, it seems—to Reaganism, to the cradle of the Greatest Generation, to the Confederacy, to Jacksonianism, and on and on.

It is no coincidence that, in response to the historical recidivism of the Trump-led right, all that the amassed forces of the Resistance™ have been able to muster is a Fukuyaman defense that, in many ways, mirrors that of their opponents. From Hillary Clinton's proclamation that "America never stopped being great" to the milquetoast Democratic obsession with being on the "right side of history," the essence of the great political slap-fight of our day seems to amount to a debate between

Democrats and Republicans over *when*, exactly—*not if*—history ended, which parts of our society are still stuck "in history," and what they need to do to catch up. Either way, the presumption is that, regardless of what happens over the next two to six years, the great historical edifice of neoliberal rule will hold.

This is why the Democratic and Never-Trump Republican resistance has been largely incapable of challenging Trump's wrecking-ball presidency on any grounds that would directly implicate the neoliberal apparatus of which they, too, are a part. Instead, the horror and hysteria unleashed by the ascendancy of Trump has been couched in pearl-clutching fear over what "norms" and "traditions" the MAGA movement has destroyed and expunged from our social world. If the neoliberal world order remains the embodied truth of the "end of history," then, for all its concerned showmanship, the neoliberal establishment has yet to demonstrate any widespread belief that history, as such, is at stake.

Perhaps this outlook is a testament to the enduring acceptance that, as the cold dust from the collapse of the Soviet Union settled, as the sun shone on the supposed "end of history," all sense of historical urgency—all sense that history is a vulnerable, perishable thing that must be fought for—hardened into concrete. In the popular mind, history became a settled matter, a taken-for-granted fixture in the background of the new millennium. Gone were the days of Marxist dialectics, Trotskyite permanent revolution, Spenglerian life cycles, the rise and fall of civilizations charted by Arnold J. Toynbee. At last history had stabilized on the model of Western liberal democracy; everything thereafter, including the Trumpian takeover of government, has been a matter of content, not form.

And yet, every day, all around us, the very meaning of history is eroding and dissipating. On the barren shores at the end of history, even the victors wander like historical amnesiacs. From within the worldwide windowless enclosure of the neoliberal order, the circuits of historical memory are frying, history itself has begun to break apart, and the end of the end may be in sight.

HISTORY IS ONLY ever as good as its means of enforcement. From our perch at the "end of history," how we remember the past, and the role it plays in justifying the shape of the present, has been routinely secured and enforced by the fact of global neoliberal domination itself. The continuance of this domination is supposed to serve as proof that history has always been leading to this point and has nowhere to go from here. This vision of history, of course, has also been buttressed by a largely unchallenged arrangement of officialized cultural institutions, disciplinary practices, standards of expertise, and sanctified narratives of national progress, all of which have served to reproduce and reinforce notions of a settled history whose archive could always be expanded with new knowledge but whose regime of truth could never be upended.

But what good is this historical vision in a world where history as such has been unmoored and set adrift in the fickle, boiling rapids of the perpetual present? What security does history provide for the neoliberal status quo when the apparatuses of memory—from those officialized cultural institutions and practices to our own internal capacity for long-term historical consciousness—are the subject and the instrument of twenty-first-century political warfare?

As we are dragged further down the cragged gullet of the new millennium, we are experiencing more and more what it means to live and politick in a world in which the stilled machine of history has rusted under the monstrous weight of the permanent now. After all, these are the very circumstances in which Trump-style politics has thrived, moving seamlessly in the taken-for-grantedness of a land- and mind-scape that is increasingly dominated by digital technologies, and that has made history itself (and historical memory) more malleable than ever before. The reactionary Trump style, that is, has proven far more adept at navigating a political world that has adjusted to the fact that we are suspended in a hypermediated connection to an eternal present, in a permanent state of anxious distraction, bombarded by the new, the spectacular, and the self-affirming.

Moving within the slippery circuitry of such a world, Trump himself has become immune to the sting of his own history. He never pauses long enough to let history crush him; he and his administration just keep piling on more controversies, gaffs, lies, and atrocities. And, for our part, as we are forced to always be playing catch up, as we struggle to keep our heads above water in the flooded present, we become increasingly susceptible to forgetting what just passed, let alone holding anyone accountable for it.

It is no coincidence that the Trump-led right has harnessed this history-resistant style of politics to launch an all-out assault on history as we know it. From Trump's never-ending lies and attacks on the media to the GOP's ramped-up war on academia, from white supremacist rallies defending Confederate monuments to conservative pundits discounting the role of slavery in the Civil War, there is, indeed, a war going on over the terrain of remembrance and over the mechanisms for enforcing history. Whether one considers the best-selling historical revisionism of Dinesh D'Souza, the weaponized falsehoods broadcast on Fox News, the power of erasure and censorship held by the titans of Big Tech, or ideologically warped narratives approved for K–12 history books, the fact that traces of these and other noxious forces are being sucked up and reproduced

Alvarez

at the level of policy in the country's highest offices is a clear sign that the battle for history is still on.

And yet many of us, especially those in the ranks of the so-called resistance, routinely confront this reality with a cavalier, Fukuyaman confidence that this, too, shall pass, that "sanity" will eventually be "restored," and that history will stand stalwart witness, attesting to future generations that we were on the "right side." But can we honestly, and with certainty, say that history—as we know it, and as we are capable of knowing it—will still be there? Can we rest assured that the end of history will sustain itself, even if history cannot?

We are now fighting on terrains where the old rules of historical warfare no longer apply. In the hypermediated reality of an endless political now, the meaning of history is determined and enforced not by the myriad monuments reminding us of our past, but by those who employ enough blunt force to occupy our attention in the present. What this will mean for the "end of history" is by no means clear. For history, though, only the old truth holds: you've got to fight for it.

Banking on the Cold War

Nikhil Pal Singh

ON SEPTEMBER 21, 1945—five months after Franklin Roosevelt's death—
President Harry Truman assembled his cabinet for a meeting that one
historian has called "a turning point in the American century." The purpose
of the meeting was to discuss Secretary of War Henry Stimson's proposal
to share atomic bomb information with the Soviets. Stimson, who had
directed the Manhattan Project, maintained that the only way to make
the Soviets trustworthy was to trust them. In his proposal to Truman, he
wrote that not sharing the bomb with the Soviets would "almost certainly
stimulate feverish activity on the part of the Soviets . . . in what will in
effect be a secret armament race of a rather desperate character."

Henry Wallace, the secretary of commerce and former vice president,
agreed with Stimson, as did Undersecretary of State Dean Acheson (though
he later changed his position), but Secretary of the Navy James Forrestal
laid down the definitive opposition. "The Russians, like the Japanese," he
argued, "are essentially Oriental in their thinking, and until we have a
longer record of experience with them . . . it seems doubtful that we should
endeavor to buy their understanding and sympathy. We tried that once

with Hitler. There are no returns on appeasement." Forrestal, a skilled bureaucratic infighter, had made his fortune on Wall Street and frequently framed his arguments in economic terms. The bomb and the knowledge that produced it, Forrestal argued, was "the property of the American people"—control over it, like the U.S. seizure of Japan's former Pacific Island bases, needed to be governed by the concept of "sole Trusteeship."

Truman sided with Forrestal. Stimson retired that very same day, his swan song ignored, and Wallace, soon to be forced out of the Truman administration for his left-wing views, described the meeting as "one of the most dramatic of all cabinet meetings in my fourteen years of Washington experience." Forrestal, meanwhile, went on to be the country's first secretary of defense in 1947 and is the man who illustrates perhaps more than anyone else how Cold War militarism achieved its own coherence and legitimacy by adopting economic logic and criteria—that is, by envisioning military power as an independent domain of capital expenditure in the service of a political economy of freedom. From his pivotal work in logistics and procurement during World War II, to his assiduously cultivated relationships with anti–New Deal congressmen and regional business leaders sympathetic to the military, Forrestal both helped to fashion and occupied the nexus of an emerging corporate-military order. He only served as defense secretary for eighteen months (he committed suicide under suspicious circumstances in 1949), but on the day of that fateful cabinet meeting, he won the decisive battle, advocating for what he once called a state of ongoing "semi-war."

The post–World War II rise of a U.S. military-industrial complex is well understood, but it still remains hidden in plain sight. Today warnings about Donald Trump's assault on the "liberal international order" are commonplace while less examined is how we arrived at a point where democratic and "peacetime" governance entails a global military infrastructure of 800 U.S. military bases in more than 70 countries.

Moreover, this infrastructure is under the command of one person, supported by a labor force numbering in the millions, and oriented to a more-or-less permanent state of war. If a politics of threat inflation and fear is one part of the answer, the other, more prosaic component is that the system itself is modeled after the scope of business and finance. By managing a diverse portfolio of assets and liabilities and identifying investment opportunities, it envisions a preeminently destructive enterprise as a series of returns calibrated to discretionary assessment of threats and a preponderance of force. This was Forrestal's bailiwick.

A LITTLE-KNOWN ANECDOTE about Truman's 1947 call to Congress for decisive intervention in the Greek civil war—generally viewed as the official declaration of the Cold War—illustrates this point. Truman's speech is famous for its emphasis on political freedom, particularly the idea of protecting peoples' rights to self-determination against "armed minorities"—"the terrorist activities of several thousand armed men, led by communists." "One of the primary objectives of the foreign policy of the United States," Truman said, establishing the characteristic linkage between World War II and the Cold War, "is the creation of conditions in which we and other nations will be able to work out a way of life free from coercion. . . . Our victory was won over countries which sought to impose their will, and their way of life, upon other nations."

The moral and rhetorical heightening of the opposition between democracy and communism (and, incipiently, terrorism) was a conscious choice. Truman was famously advised by Republican senator Arthur Vandenburg that securing public and congressional support for unprecedented and costly peacetime intervention into European affairs entailed "scaring the hell out of the American people." Another, less visible choice, however,

Singh

was to downplay the role of the accountant's ledger, which was more overt in an early draft of Truman's speech. That draft argued that emergency financial support for Greece (and Turkey) was now a requirement of world capitalism: "Two great wars and an intervening world depression have weakened the [capitalist] system almost everywhere except in the United States. If, by default, we permit free enterprise to disappear in other countries of the world, the very existence of our democracy will be gravely threatened." Acknowledging the less-than-compelling purchase of this argument, Secretary of State Dean Acheson remarked derisively that it made "the whole thing sound like an investment prospectus."

Truman's delivered address, by contrast, made use of the words "free" and "freedom" twenty-four times in a few minutes, as if talismanic repetition were enough to hinge the defense of private capital accumulation to the maintenance of popular democracy the world over. Yet, despite the inflated rhetoric, economic considerations remained the skeletal core of the Truman Doctrine. Buried inside the address was the acknowledged collapse of British imperial policy in the region, along with an "invitation" from a dubiously democratic, right-wing Greek government for "financial and other assistance" in support of "better public administration." The imperatives of democracy and self-government—preeminent political values understood by the U.S. public—were subordinated to building "an economy in which a healthy democracy can flourish." In a final nod to the bean counters, Truman noted that the amount he was requesting was a mere fraction of what the United States spent during World War II, and no less justified as "an investment in world freedom and world peace."

The challenge for U.S. policy makers going forward was to reconcile a lofty rhetorical and moral emphasis upon the principle of political self-determination with the necessity of investing military force (i.e., "other assistance") whose paramount end was securing the market freedoms of national and international capitalists. The teleological (and tautological) proposition that a substratum of properly capitalist economic relations organically yielded a democratic harvest would be the farmer's almanac of a rising generation of modernization theorists. But the reality on the ground—in a world where the main provenance of self-determination was defined by the bloody rearguard defense of colonial prerogatives on the part of the United States' most important allies and industrial partners—was bitter, and far less susceptible to universalizing nostrums. Straight-talking U.S. policy makers, particularly those at the center of the military apparatus, knew it.

The following year, for example, George Kennan, author of the "containment" doctrine, a protégé of Forrestal, and the single most influential strategic foreign policy thinker of the moment, offered a strikingly candid version of the task at hand, in a classified memo that consciously punctured the universalist ambit of the Truman Doctrine:

> We have about 50% of the world's wealth but only 6.3% of its population. This disparity is particularly great as between ourselves and the peoples of Asia. In this situation, we cannot fail to be the object of envy and resentment. Our real task in the coming period is to *devise a pattern of relationships which will permit us to maintain this position of disparity without positive detriment to our security*. To do so, we will have to dispense with all sentimentality and day-dreaming; and our attention will have to be concentrated everywhere on our immediate national objectives. We need not deceive ourselves that we can afford today the luxury of altruism and world-benefaction. (emphasis added)

When thinking about nations and peoples, particularly those outside of Europe, Kennan again foregrounded a logic of investment and risk management, and he advised restraint and limitation of liability, especially with respect to "the peoples of Asia . . . [who] are going to go ahead, whatever we do, with the development of their political forms and mutual interrelationships in their own way." Kennan warned that the coming

Singh

period would be neither "liberal" nor "peaceful," and that such countries were likely to "fall, for varying periods, under the influence of Moscow, whose ideology has a greater lure for such peoples, and probably greater reality, than anything we could oppose to it . . . [or that] our people would ever willingly concede to such a purpose." In this light, he concluded that the United States needed to dispense with commitments, rhetorical and otherwise, to "unreal objectives such as human rights, the raising of living standards, and democratization. The day is not far off when we are going to have to deal in straight power concepts."

This view is sometimes depicted as an exemplary instance of realism—wiser and more in tune with the messy, uneven world that emerged from World War II—and a point of view that, had it been heeded, may have prevented the costly overreach of global cold war, especially "blunders" such as the Vietnam War (which Kennan, long retired to academia, opposed). The concept of realism, however, fails to grasp the functional logic of risk and threat assessment—the insistent and anxious hedging and speculation that made the careers and fortunes of Kennan, Forrestal, and many that followed them. Forrestal fretted obsessively in his diary along these lines: "I am more impressed than ever as things develop in the world today that policy may be frequently shaped by events unless someone has a strong and clear mental grasp of events; strong enough and clear enough so that he is able to shape policy rather than letting it be developed by accidents." This recurrent epistemic anxiety initiated an insistent demand for anticipatory policy, abiding mistrust, and the maintenance of a preponderance of force. As Forrestal bluntly put it, "Power is needed until we are sure of the reign of law."

Despite his long period of service within a New Deal liberal political milieu, Forrestal (like Kennan) was disinterested in universalizing the scope of political self-determination overseas, recognizing as more pressing the preservation of a capitalist economy built on uneven development and asymmetric military power at a world scale. Electrified upon reading Kennan's "Long Telegram" (1946), Forrestal viewed his fellow Princeton man as a kindred soul, one who had intuited similar grounds of Orientalist menace, inscrutability, and immunity to anything but the language of force in Soviet conduct. It was Forrestal who brought Kennan to Washington, D.C., from Moscow and into the policy-making apparatus; both men were solicitous toward the value of rank and privilege, tolerant of authoritarian deviations from liberal standards, and assured that freedom from coercion was the provenance of those who, in Kennan's words, were already imbued with "Anglo-Saxon traditions of compromise."

Forrestal framed his own deference for hierarchy in terms of the prerogatives of corporate capitalism—the idea that practical men of business, rather than reformers and intellectuals, had won World War II and needed to be running the world going forward. Among his more forceful conclusions was that liberal globalism would be disastrous if it were not steeled with counterrevolutionary animus. As he confided to diplomat Stanton Griffiths:

> Between Hitler, your friends to the east, and the intellectual muddlers who have had the throttle for the last ten years, the practical people are going to have a hell of a time getting the world out of receivership, and when the miracles are not produced the crackpots may demand another chance in which to really finish the job. At that time, it will be of greatest importance that the Democratic Party speaks for the liberals, but not for the revolutionaries.

For these realists, even more than the wooly moralists they sometimes ridiculed, it was the credibility of U.S. threats of force that ensured the freedom and mobility of productive capital and supported its resource needs and allied interests across an ever-widening sphere. Of a more aristocratic and consciously anti-democratic mien, Kennan likewise recognized that the animating logic was not strictly anti-communist but counterrevolutionary—indeed even racial. The inevitable dissolution of the colonial system meant that the challenge of U.S. policy in the coming period was broader than the struggle with Soviet communism, as "all persons with grievances, whether economic or racial will be urged to seek redress not in mediation and compromise, but in defiant, violent struggle." Inspired by communist appeals, "poor will be set against rich, black against white, young against old, newcomers against established residents."

BY ELIDING SOVIET DESIGNS with those of heterogeneous movements demanding effective sovereignty and challenging material deprivation, Forrestal and his colleagues contributed to a perverse recasting of the dynamic of European colonial disintegration as the field of Soviet imperial expansion. This rhetorical and ideological frame practically demanded the militarization of U.S. foreign policy, with U.S. "counter-force" the only alternative to a world *ruled by force*. As such, along with Arthur Radford, Forrestal was instrumental in developing the Central Intelligence Agency (CIA), and that agency's work soon echoed his. In 1948, for instance, a CIA document entitled "The Break-Up of Colonial Empires and its Implications for US Security" defined expressions of "economic nationalism" and "racial antagonism" as primary sources of "friction between the colonial powers and the US on the one hand, and the states of the Near and Far East on the other."

The CIA's analysts suggested that poverty and a legacy of anti-colonial grievances rendered colonized and formerly colonized peoples "peculiarly susceptible to Soviet penetration" and warned that the "gravest danger" facing the United States was that decolonizing nations might fall into alignment with the USSR. At the same time, they faulted Europe's colonial powers for their failure to satisfy "the aspirations of their dependent areas" and advised them to "devise formulae that will retain their good will as emergent or independent states." Envisioning U.S. responsibility to author such formulae in the future, the classified brief concluded that the United States should adopt "a more positive and sympathetic attitude toward the national aspirations of these areas," including policy that "at least partially meets their demands for economic assistance." Otherwise "it will risk their becoming actively antagonistic toward the US," including loss of access to previously "assured sources of raw materials, markets, and military bases."

While the emerging U.S. foreign policy clearly accepted the un-resolvable antagonism toward the Soviet Union, the challenge of the future, as the CIA argued, was how the United States should address the "increasing fragmentation of the non-Soviet world," or, in a word, decolonization. The means for assessing risk and reward in this expansive and heterogeneous terrain of imperial disintegration were by no means clear. But it is revealing that the possibility of potential alignments be-tween decolonizing nations and Soviet power was far less concrete and worrisome to the United States than the more definite and delineated material losses faced by the United States and the colonial powers with which it had aligned itself—namely, being deprived access to formerly "assured sources of raw materials, markets and military bases." In other words, the challenge of the future, as Kennan had underlined, was to devise "formulae" to buttress the forms of political authority that sustained economic inequality (at a world scale) in the face of inevitable revolt and revolution against such authority and the social conditions it supported.

Despite his later misgivings, Kennan had authored the concept whose rhetorical elasticity and ideological indeterminacy proved crucial to fashioning a nemesis that suited this consciously expansionist vision of U.S. economic and military power. With the creation of the CIA, the

National Security Council, and Forrestal's own new position of secretary of defense, these years saw the growth of a national security bureaucracy that was divorced from meaningful oversight and public accountability for its actions, including myriad moral failures and calamities. A covert anti-Soviet destabilization campaign in Eastern Europe, for example, greenlit by Forrestal and Kennan, enlisted Ukrainian partisans who had worked with the Nazis. This type of activity would become routine in Latin America, Asia, and Africa, where Kennan derided respect for the "delicate fiction of sovereignty" that undeserving, "unprepared peoples" had been allowed to extend over the resources of the earth.

OVER THE NEXT quarter century, fewer than 400 individuals operated the national security bureaucracy, with some individuals enjoying decades of influence. That the top tier was dominated by white men who were Ivy League–educated lawyers, bankers, and corporate executives (often with ties to armament-related industries) lends irony to official fearmongering about armed conspiracies mounted by small groups, let alone the idea that the role of the United States was to defend free choice against coercion imposed by nonrepresentative minorities. This fact, perhaps more than any other, suggests that, as much as the Cold War represented a competition between incompatible, if by no means coeval or equally powerful systems of rule (i.e., communist and capitalist), it was marked by convergences too. The Soviet "empire of justice" and the U.S. "empire of liberty" engaged in mimetic, cross-national interventions, clandestine, counter-subversive maneuvers, and forms of clientelism that were all dictated by elite, ideologically cohesive national security bureaucracies immune from popular scrutiny and democratic oversight.

Those charged with governing the controlling seat of U.S. globalism consistently doubted the compatibility of normative democratic requirements and the security challenges they envisioned, including distrust that often bordered on contempt for the publics in whose name they claimed to act. "We are today in the midst of a cold war, our enemies are to be found abroad and at home," remarked Bernard Baruch, coining the term that names this era. In this context, "the survival of the state is not a matter of law," Acheson famously declared, an argument similar to one being advanced by former Nazi jurist Carl Schmitt. Vandenberg, echoing defenders of Roosevelt's accretive accumulation of war powers, was positively wistful lamenting "the heavy handicap" that the United States faced "when imperiled by an autocracy like Russia where decisions require nothing but a narrow Executive mandate." For Forrestal, "the most dangerous spot is our own country because the people are so eager for peace and have such a distaste for war that they will grasp for any sign of a solution of a problem that has had them deeply worried."

Forrestal felt that the danger at home manifested itself most frustratingly in the threat that congressional budgeting posed to military requirements. The preservation of a state of peace was a costly proposition when it revolved around open-ended threat prevention the world over. Upholding the permanent preponderance of U.S. military power at a global scale required a new type of fiscal imagination, one that had to be funded by the future promise of tax receipts. During his final year in office, Forrestal's diary records in mind-numbing detail his worries about acquiring Pentagon funding adequate to his projections for global military reach. In Forrestal's view, budgetary considerations were captive to the wrong baseline of "peak of war danger" and combatting "aggression" rather than to "maintenance of a permanent state of adequate military preparation."

A fascinating aspect of these budget wrangles is Forrestal's manic efforts to translate future-oriented geostrategic needs into precise dollar values. Just months before his forced retirement and eventual suicide, he confided to Walter G. Andrews:

> Our biggest headache at the moment, of course, is the budget. The President has set the ceiling at 14 billion 4 against the pared down requirements that we put in of 16 billion 9. I am frank to say, however, I have the greatest sympathy with him because he is determined not to spend more than we take in in taxes. He is a hard-money man if ever I saw one.

Despite his grudging admiration for the stolid Truman, Forrestal's Wall Street background had left him at ease in a more speculative or liquid universe; at that precise moment, he was devising accounting gimmicks to offset near billion-dollar costs of stockpiling raw materials as a "capital item" that could be "removed from the budget." The important point to emphasize is the relationship between two interrelated forms of speculation and accounting—economic and military—in which an absolute inflation of threats tempted a final break with lingering hard-money orthodoxies and a turn to deficit spending. Forrestal did not live to see the breakthrough, but his work paid off.

As Acheson described it, the Korean War—the first hot war of the Cold War era—"saved" the fledgling national security state. With its outbreak, the dream of eternal military liquidity was realized when Leon Keyserling, the liberal economist serving as Truman's chairman of the Council of Economic Advisors, argued that military expenditures functioned as an economic growth engine. That theory then underpinned NSC 68, the document that justified massive U.S. defense outlays for the foreseeable future and which was authored by another Forrestal protégé, Paul Nitze. By yoking dramatically increased federal spending to security prerogatives, *military* Keynesianism thus achieved a permanent augmentation of U.S. state capacity no longer achievable under appeals to Keynesianism alone.

THE EMBEDDING OF the global priorities of a national security state, which sometimes appears inevitable in retrospect, was by no means assured in the years leading up to the Korean War. It was challenged by uncooperative allies, a war-weary or recalcitrant U.S. public, and politicians who were willing to cede U.S. military primacy and security prerogatives in the name of international cooperation. But by 1947, men such as Forrestal had laid the groundwork for rejecting the Rooseveltian internationalist inheritance, arguing it was necessary to "accept the fact that the concept of one world upon which the United Nations was based is no longer valid and that we are in political fact facing a division into two worlds." Although the militarization of U.S. policy is often understood to have been reactive and conditioned by threats from the outside, his ruminations illustrate how militarized globalism was actively conceived as anticipatory policy (in advance of direct confrontations with the Soviet Union) by just a few architects and defense intellectuals—men under whose sway we continue to live and die.

Ultimately, the declaration of the Cold War says more about how these U.S. elites represented and imagined their "freedom" and envisioned the wider world as a domain for their own discretionary action and accumulation than it did about enabling other people to be free, let alone shaping the terms of a durable and peaceful international order. As early as 1946, Forrestal began taking important businessmen on tours of the wreckage of Pacific Island battles, which also happened to be future sites for U.S. nuclear testing. Forestall described these ventures as "an effort to provide long-term insurance against the disarmament wave, the shadows of which I can already see peeping over the horizon." The future of the bomb and the empire of bases were already on his mind.

Forrestal recognized that force and threat are always fungible things to be leveraged in the service of the reality that truly interested him, the reality made by men who own the future. For those of his cast of mind, "international order" was never more than the fig leaf of wealth and power. As he noted in a 1948 letter to Hansen Baldwin of the *New York Times*: "It has long been one of my strongly held beliefs that the word 'security' ought to be stricken from the language, and the word 'risk' substituted. I came to that conclusion out of my own business experience." It was the job, after all, of these East Coast lawyers and moneymen to make sure all bets were hedged, and Forrestal knew that speculation could turn into "an investment gone bad." As a leading investor in the Cold War project, he wanted a guaranteed return, even if the rule of law never arrived and even when the price was ruin.

The Welfare World

Adom Getachew

IN 1972 THE SOCIALIST LEFT swept to power in Jamaica. Calling for the strengthening of workers' rights, the nationalization of industries, and the expansion of the island's welfare state, the People's National Party (PNP), led by the charismatic Michael Manley, sought nothing less than to overturn the old order under which Jamaicans had long labored—first as enslaved, then indentured, then colonized, and only recently as politically free of Great Britain. Jamaica is a small island, but the ambition of the project was global in scale.

Two years before his election as prime minister, Manley took to the pages of *Foreign Affairs* to situate his democratic socialism within a novel account of international relations. While the largely North Atlantic readers of the magazine might have identified the fissures of the Cold War as the dominant conflict of their time, Manley argued otherwise. The "real battleground," he declared, was located "in that largely tropical territory which was first the object of colonial exploitation, second, the focus of non-Caucasian nationalism and more latterly known as the underdeveloped and the developing world as it sought euphemisms for its condition." Manley displaced the Cold War's East–West divide, instead drawing on a longstanding anti-colonial critique to look at the world along its North–South axis. When viewed from the "tropics," the world was not bifurcated by ideology, but by a global economy whose origins lay in the project of European imperial expansion.

Imperialism, for Manley, was a form of not just political but *economic* domination through which territories such as Jamaica were "geared to produce not what was needed for themselves or for exchange for mutual advantage, but rather . . . compelled to be the producers of what others needed." Between the 1940s and '60s, the first generation of anti-co-lonial nationalists, including Norman Manley, Michael's father, had largely liberated their countries from the *political* chains of empire by securing independence. Anti-colonial nationalists aspired to use their newfound sovereignty to transform the political and economic legacies of imperialism. As a member of the second generation of postwar na-tionalists, Manley viewed his election as an opportunity to realize this aspiration for postcolonial transformation. Given "the condition of a newly independent society encumbered with the economic, social and psychological consequences of three hundred years of colonialism," Man-ley hoped his political program would secure "individual and collective self-reliance" as well as political and economic equality. His platform of democratic socialism for Jamaica inaugurated an ambitious project of land redistribution, state control of key industries, stronger rights for organized labor, worker ownership of industries, and the expansion of health care and education.

However, this vision of postcolonial transformation was limited by the very forms of dependence and inequality that it sought to overcome. Because postcolonial states remained primary good exporters with na-tional economies dependent on products such as bauxite, cocoa, coffee, cotton, sisal, and tea, their domestic economic policies were subject to the vagaries of the international market. This contradiction between the achievement of political sovereignty and the persistence of economic dependence, famously captured in Kwame Nkrumah's term *neocolonialism*, was heightened as Manley inaugurated his socialist project. Already beginning in the late 1960s, prices for primary products in international markets experienced a precipitous decline. Coupled with OPEC's 1973 oil embargo, which heavily burdened new postcolonial states dependent on oil imports, the decline in commodity prices resulted in steep foreign exchange shortages and exacerbated postcolonial states' reliance on debt.

The end of this story is a familiar one. By the 1980s, unable to service their debt, postcolonial states entered structural adjustment agreements with the World Bank and International Monetary Fund (IMF). While Mexico's 1982 default is often viewed as the beginning of this process, Manley's Jamaica was the first victim of the Third World debt crisis and began structural adjustment in 1977. Then in his second term, Manley acceded to the terms of the IMF's stabilization program, which required a 30 percent devaluation of Jamaica's currency; major cuts in public expenditures, especially in the wages of public sector workers; and the privatization of state assets. Long before Greece's SYRIZA, there was Manley and his PNP.

ALTHOUGH THE 1970s ended with postcolonial capitulation to the new age of neoliberal globalization, the decade had begun on a very different note: with a radical call from the Global South for a New International Economic Order (NIEO). Announced in the UN General Assembly with the Declaration on the Establishment of a New International Economic Order (1974) and the Charter of Economic Rights and Duties of States (1974), the NIEO was conceived as the international corollary to the domestic projects of socialism Manley and other anti-colonial nationalists were pursuing. How did such an ambitious effort—to create an egalitarian global economy—emerge?

A decade prior to passage of the Declaration on the Establishment of the NEIO and the Charter on Economic Rights and Duties of States, the Afro-Asian bloc of states in the United Nations had come to recognize a possible source of strength in their majority in the General Assembly. They mobilized to create the United Nations Conference of Trade and Development (UNCTAD). Unlike the World Bank and IMF, which were created prior to the postwar surge of decolonization and empowered states of the Global North, UNCTAD was organized as a forum to address trade and development in the Global South. Despite the opposition of the United States and its allies, Third World states used their majority to place the Argentine economist and dependency theorist Raúl Prebisch at the helm of this new agency. It was in UNCTAD, and then on the floor of the UN General Assembly, that the policy prescriptions of the NIEO were first articulated and backed by a group of Third World states that had organized themselves under the name G-77. In its ambition to transform international economic relations, the NIEO addressed critical issues that included the ownership of resources in land, space, and the seas; the growing power of transnational corporations; and the transportation of goods in an increasingly globalized commodity chain. At its core, however, the NIEO was concerned with the unequal relations of trade between the Global North and South. Proponents of the NIEO saw in this inequality a distorted and damaging international division of labor, one that, according to Manley, consistently relegated postcolonial states to "the low end of the 'value added' scale." Until something changed, they would be condemned to serve as "planter and reaper," economically subservient to the Global North with its manufacturing economies, high incomes, and domestic consumer markets.

To overcome the dependence that structured international trade, UNCTAD and the postcolonial statesmen who supported the NIEO looked for lessons in the welfare states of the twentieth century. These systems, constructed by the labor movements of industrialized societies, were by the 1970s at the peak of their success in diminishing domestic inequality. The assumption that an egalitarian global economy could be modeled on the welfare state thus depended on viewing the position of postcolonial states as structurally analogous to the working class and rural sector within the states of the Global North. This analogy, transposing from the domestic political economies of the Global North to the political economy of the whole planet, shaped the politics of the NIEO in two ways.

First, it framed Third World solidarity as an assertive class politics. As Manley noted, the postcolonial world "now proclaimed itself the Third World to mark its transition from an age of apology to one of assertiveness." According to Julius Nyerere, president of Tanzania and one of Manley's collaborators, postcolonial states had constituted themselves as an international "trade union of the poor." The G-77 in the UN General Assembly—as well as commodity associations modelled on OPEC that would negotiate the price of products such as bauxite and coffee—were manifestations of this trade unionism. Like the labor movements of the nineteenth and twentieth centuries, their demand for economic equality was predicated on the view that the postcolonial world had produced the wealth that the Global North enjoyed. In this recasting of economic relations between the Global North and South, the NIEO's proponents reimagined the international arena as a site for a politics of redistribution that extended far beyond the discourses of aid and charity.

Second, the domestic analogy cast the postcolonial project as an effort to internationalize the postwar social compact between labor and capital. The NIEO was, to use Gunnar Myrdal's term, a "welfare world" that would democratize global economic decision-making and redistribute the gains of global trade. In the absence of a world state armed with the coercive power of taxation, this international welfarism sought to deploy the United Nations to regulate market prices of primary commodities, provide compensatory financing when prices fell unexpectedly, remove protectionist barriers in the Global North, and provide "special and preferential treatment" for the products postcolonial states produced. UNCTAD justified this set of policy prescriptions by insisting that the international community had "a clear responsibility towards developing countries that have suffered a deterioration in their terms of trade in the same way as Governments recognize a similar responsibility towards their domestic primary producers." This responsibility was not framed as a rectification or reparation for past injustices of the global economy. Instead, it was a claim that internationalizing the welfare state was necessary for overcoming the structural inequality of global trade—and thereby, for achieving a postimperial global economy. Just as the workers' movements of the Global North had, in their struggles for unions and socialism, built democracy in Germany, Britain, France, and the United States, so too would the states of the Global South, in pursuing global economic equality, achieve a new world political order.

The welfare world of the NIEO marked the high point of anticolonial politics in the United Nations and indicated a sharp break with the postwar status quo. If the right to self-determination had universalized legal equality for postcolonial states, the NIEO radicalized the meaning of sovereign equality. In the hands of postcolonial states, sovereign equality now entailed equal decision-making power within the United Nations. According to the Charter of Rights and Duties, the juridical equality of all states and their equal status as members of the international community granted them "the right to participate fully and effectively in the international decision-making process in the solution of world economic, financial and monetary problems." This claim of equal legislative power grounded the more ambitious claim that sovereign equality had material implications: it required and entailed an equitable share of the world's wealth. According to the Declaration on the Establishment of the NIEO, the welfare world aimed for "the broadest co-operation of all the States members of the international community, based on equity, whereby the prevailing disparities in the world may be banished and prosperity secured for all."

Fearing that Third World states would launch commodity embargoes on the model of OPEC's 1973 oil embargo, Western statesmen initially pursued a conciliatory policy of appeasement in public even as they criticized the NIEO privately. In this context, postcolonial states gained allies among social democrats in the Global North and secured small victories. For instance, with the addition of Part 4 to the General Agreement on Trade and Tariffs, postcolonial states were able to secure lower tariffs in the Global North on some of their goods. Moreover, postcolonial states were freed from the requirement of reciprocity in trade agreements with the Global North. These special and preferential provisions recognized the unfair character of international trade and sought to strengthen the position of postcolonial states.

However, the political openings that made possible these concessions and enabled the Third World to demand the NIEO proved narrow. With commodity prices declining and debt skyrocketing, the bargaining power of postcolonial states eroded rapidly. By the end of the 1970s, the era of neoliberal globalization had dawned, displacing visions of a welfare world. Leading the opposition to the NIEO, the World Bank and IMF rejected its aspiration to democratic and universal international economic law. Instead, these financial institutions insulated the global economy from political contestation by recasting it as the domain of technocratic expertise. In doing so, they rejected the claim that the global economy could be subject to demands for redistribution. The colony went free, stood for a brief moment in the sun, then moved back again toward servitude—this time to the empire of debt.

ALMOST FORTY YEARS after the triumph of neoliberalism over the NIEO, it is difficult to imagine that another world was possible. In accepting this triumph as inevitable, we have forgotten that decolonization promised not only to free nations from foreign domination, but also to remake the world. From our perspective, the wave of independence movements that followed World War II is largely associated with the moral and legal delegitimization of alien rule, the transition from colony to nation, and the expansion of the international society to include previously excluded African, Asian, and Caribbean states. In this view, anti-colonial nationalists appropriated the principle of self-determination and the modular form of the nation-state, expanding and universalizing languages and institutions with a European provenance.

This is a compelling narrative because it describes the world that emerged from decolonization. In the three decades between 1945 and 1975, UN membership had grown from 51 states to 144. At the turn of the twentieth century, European states ruled 84 percent of Earth's surface; by 1975 the remnants of alien rule, largely in southern Africa, appeared to be anachronistic and barbaric holdouts. However, this narrative obscures some of the most innovative aspects of the politics of decolonization by eliding its global ambitions. And it thereby misses the mechanisms by which empire reasserted itself, persisting into our time and reinforcing global white supremacy.

When African and West Indian nationalists met at the Fifth Pan-African Congress in Manchester in 1945 to articulate a global vision of decolonization, national independence was high on their agenda. But it was only one part of an internationalist framework that looked forward to "inevitable world unity and federation." From Ghana's Nkrumah, who helped to organize the Pan-African Congress, to Jamaica's Manley, anti-colonial nationalists pitched decolonization on this *global* scale to address the global character of imperialism. In their view, empire was a globalizing force that unequally and violently integrated disparate peoples and lands. With the gun and the lash, it had made a single world from many. It produced, according to W. E. B. Du Bois, a global color line through which Europe dominated the "darker . . . races of men in Asia and Africa, in America and the islands of the sea." This structure of racial hierarchy endured well after the achievement of juridical independence, finding a new form in Manley's "real battleground," which demarcated the postcolonial world and the Global North.

Seeking to undo international economic hierarchies and shore up the right to self-determination, the NIEO sought to realize the aspiration to "world unity and federation" by creating international frameworks that would support self-rule at home. This novel combination of nation-building and world-making—the idea that democratic self-governance depended on an international context conducive to its exercise—emerged out of the sense that empire's globalization could be made egalitarian but could not be reversed. The world was already unified, under the terms of white supremacy and capitalist exploitation. As Manley pointed out, the Caribbean itself was a global formation and could not be disaggregated from the international political and economic relations in which it was embedded. This extreme form of extraversion necessarily required moving beyond national insularity.

Getachew

The ideal of a national independence disembedded from the world was not only a fantasy for decolonizing nations—it was also increasingly impossible for the Global North. Anticipating the contemporary dilemmas of neoliberal globalization, Manley argued that international entanglements of trade, capital flows, and financialization, as well as the emergence of transnational private actors, threatened to undermine the capacity of all states to steer and regulate their national economies. For Manley, the multinational corporation revealed the growing contradictions between the international economy and the bounded nation-state. In creating an international system of political management for the world economy, the NIEO would supplement the diminished role of the state. It would create a system for political and democratic regulation of the global economy, ultimately benefiting all states and peoples. Thus while anticolonial nationalists reimagined international institutions for the postcolonial condition, their vision extended beyond the Global South.

THE DEMOCRATIC DECISION-MAKING and global redistribution at the heart of the NIEO could yet again be a source for inspiration, especially in our present moment when the tension between nationalism and internationalism electrifies political debate. Brexit, the election of Donald Trump, and the wave of authoritarian populism surging across the West all frame national insularity as the solution to an age of neoliberal globalization. By withdrawing from international institutions, erecting barriers to global trade, and closing borders to migrants, the new right in the Global North aspires to realize a vision of national independence that Manley and other anti-colonial nationalists already realized was impossible fifty years ago. But if the right's model of national insularity is impossible, the neoliberal globalization that displaced anti-colonial world-making, and has been the order of the day since the 1980s, is equally untenable. Its vision of an economy insulated from political contestation and its rejection of distributive justice nationally and globally have magnified inequality and contributed to the rise of the new right. One vision would insulate nation-states from the world; the other, the world from its people. In this context, demanding a return to the liberal world order—as leading scholars in international relations and international law have recently done—is an inadequate response. It obscures the ways that the illiberal backlash of our moment emerged out of the inequalities and hypocrisies of that very same system.

From our vantage point, the welfare world of the NIEO might appear utopian and unrealistic. But to dismiss the world that decolonization aspired to make is to refuse to reckon with the dilemmas we inherited from the end of empire. It is to evade our responsibility to build a world after empire. Our world, like Manley's, is characterized by a battleground of widening inequality and ongoing domination. We cannot simply recreate the 1970s vision of a welfare world, but we can take from its architects the insight that building an egalitarian and postimperial world is the only route to true democratic self-governance.

The Absurd Apocalypse

Arundhati Roy interviewed by Avni Sejpal

IN HER SECOND NOVEL, *The Ministry of Utmost Happiness* (2017),
Arundhati Roy asks, "What is the acceptable amount of blood for good
literature?" This relationship between the imagination and the stuff of
real life—violence, injustice, power—is central to Roy's writing, dating
back to her Booker Prize–winning debut novel *The God of Small Things*
(1997). For the twenty years between the release of her first and second
novels, the Indian writer has dismayed many—those who preferred that
she stick to storytelling and those who were comfortable with the turn of
global politics around 9/11—by voicing her political dissent loudly and
publicly. Her critical essays, many published in major Indian newspapers,
take on nuclear weapons, big dams, corporate globalization, India's caste
system, the rise of Hindu nationalism, the many faces of empire, and
the U.S. war machine. They have garnered both acclaim and anger. In
India Roy has often been vilified by the media, and accused of sedi-
tion, for her views on the Indian state, the corruption of the country's
courts, and India's brutal counterinsurgency in Kashmir. She has, on
one occasion, even been sent to prison for committing "contempt of

court." In spite of this, Roy remains outspoken. In this interview, she reflects on the relationship between the aesthetic and the political in her work, how to think about power, and what it means to live and write in imperial times.

AVNI SEJPAL: You once wrote that George W. Bush "achieved what writers, scholars, and activists have striven to achieve for decades. He has exposed the ducts. He has placed on full public view the working parts, the nuts and bolts of the apocalyptic apparatus of the American empire." What did you mean by this, and ten years and two presidents later, is the American empire's apocalyptic nature still so transparent?

ARUNDHATI ROY: I was referring to Bush's unnuanced and not very intelligent commentary after the events of 9/11 and in the run-up to the invasion of Afghanistan and Iraq. It exposed the thinking of the deep state in the United States. That transparency disappeared in the Obama years, as it tends to when Democrats are in power. In the Obama years, you had to ferret out information and piece it together to figure out how many bombs were being dropped and how many people were being killed, even as the acceptance speech for the Nobel Peace Prize was being eloquently delivered. However differently their domestic policies play out on home turf, it is a truism that the Democrats' foreign policy has tended to be as aggressive as that of the Republicans. But since 9/11, between Bush and Obama, how many countries have been virtually laid to waste? And now we have the era of Trump, in which we learn that *intelligence* and *nuance* are relative terms. And that W, when compared to Trump, was a serious intellectual. Now U.S. foreign policy is tweeted to the world on an hourly basis. You can't get more transparent than that. The Absurd Apocalypse. Who would have imagined that could be possible? But it is possible—more than possible—and it will be quicker in the coming if Trump makes the dreadful mistake of attacking Iran.

AS: There is a marked stylistic difference between your two novels, *The God of Small Things* and *The Ministry of Utmost Happiness*, published two decades apart. While both speak of politics and violence, the former is written in a style often described as lyrical realism. Beauty is one of its preoccupations, and it ends on a hopeful note. *The Ministry of Utmost Happiness*, on the other hand, is a more urgent, fragmented, and bleak novel, where the losses are harder to sustain. Given the dominance of lyrical realism in the postcolonial and global novel, was your stylistic choice also a statement about the need to narrate global systems of domination differently? Is the novel an indirect call to rethink representation in Indian English fiction?

AR: *The God of Small Things* and *The Ministry of Utmost Happiness* are different kinds of novels. They required different ways of telling a story. In both, the language evolved organically as I wrote them. I am not really aware of making "stylistic choices" in a conscious way. In *The God of Small Things*, I felt my way toward a language that would contain both English and Malayalam—it was the only way to tell *that* story of *that* place and *those* people. *The Ministry of Utmost Happiness* was a much riskier venture. To write it, I had to nudge the language of *The God of Small Things* off the roof of a very tall building, then rush down and gather up the shards. *The Ministry of Utmost Happiness* is written in English but imagined in many languages—Hindi, Urdu, English. . . . I wanted to try and write a novel that was not just a story told through a few characters whose lives play out against a particular backdrop. I tried to imagine the narrative form of the novel as if it were one of the great metropoles in my part of the world—ancient, modern, planned and unplanned. A story with highways and narrow alleys, old courtyards, new freeways. A story in which you would get lost and have to find your way back. A story that a reader would have to *live* inside, not consume. A story in which I tried not to walk past people without stopping for a smoke and a quick hello. One in which even the minor characters tell you their names, their stories, where they came from, and where they wish to go.

I agree, *The Ministry of Utmost Happiness* is fragmented, urgent—I love the idea of a novel written over almost ten years being urgent—but I wouldn't call it bleak. Most of the characters, after all, are ordinary folks who refuse to surrender to the bleakness that is all around them, who insist on all kinds of fragile love and humor and vulgarity, which all thrive stubbornly in the most unexpected places. In the lives of the characters in both books, love, sorrow, despair, and hope are so tightly intertwined, and so transient, I am not sure I know which novel of the two is bleaker and which more hopeful.

I don't think in some of the categories in which your question is posed to me. For example, I don't understand what a "global" novel is. I think of both my novels as so very, very local. I am surprised by how easily they have traveled across cultures and languages. Both have been translated into more than forty languages—but does that make them "global" or just universal? And then I wonder about the term *postcolonial*. I have often used it, too, but is colonialism really *post-*? Both novels, in different ways, reflect on this question. So many kinds of entrenched and unrecognized colonialisms still exist. Aren't we letting them off the hook? Even "Indian English fiction" is, on the face of it, a pretty obvious category. But what does it really mean? The boundaries of the country we call India were arbitrarily drawn by the British. What is "Indian English"? Is it different from Pakistani English or Bangladeshi

English? Kashmiri English? There are 780 languages in India, 22 of them formally "recognized." Most of our Englishes are informed by our familiarity with one or more of those languages. Hindi, Telugu, and Malayalam speakers, for example, speak English differently. The characters in my books speak in various languages, and translate for and to each other. Translation, in my writing, is a *primary* act of creation. They, as well as the author, virtually live in the language of translation. Truly, I don't think of myself as a writer of "Indian English fiction," but as a writer whose work and whose characters live in several languages. The original is in itself part translation. I feel that my fiction comes from a place that is more ancient, as well as more modern and certainly less shallow, than the concept of nations.

Is *The Ministry of Utmost Happiness* an indirect call to rethink representation in the Indian English novel? Not consciously, no. But an author's conscious intentions are only a part of what a book ends up being. When I write fiction, my only purpose is to try and build a universe through which I invite readers to walk.

AS: In addition to writing novels, you are also a prolific essayist and political activist. Do you see activism, fiction, and nonfiction as extensions of each other? Where does one begin and the other end for you?

AR: I am not sure I have the stubborn, unwavering relentlessness it takes to make a good activist. I think that "writer" more or less covers what I do. I don't actually see my fiction and nonfiction as extensions of each other. They are pretty separate. When I write fiction, I take my time. It is leisurely, unhurried, and it gives me immense pleasure. As I said, I try to create a universe for readers to walk through.

The essays are always urgent interventions in a situation that is closing down on people. They are arguments, pleas, to look at something differently. My first political essay, "The End of Imagination," was written after India's 1998 nuclear tests. The second, "The Greater Common Good," came after the Supreme Court lifted its stay on the building of the Sardar Sarovar Dam on the Narmada River. I didn't know that they were just the beginning of what would turn out to be twenty years of essay writing. Those years of writing, traveling, arguing, being hauled up by courts, and even going to prison deepened my understanding of the land I lived in and the people I lived among, in ways I could not have imagined. That understanding built up inside me, layer upon layer.

Had I not lived those twenty years the way I did, I would not have been able to write *The Ministry of Utmost Happiness*. But when I write fiction, unlike when I write political essays, I don't write from a place of logic, reason, argument, fact. The fiction comes from years of contemplating that lived experience, turning it over and over until it appears on my skin like sweat. I write fiction with my skin. By the time I started to write *The Ministry of Utmost Happiness*, I felt like a sedimentary rock trying to turn itself into a novel.

AS: The word "empire" has often been invoked as a uniquely European and U.S. problem. Do you see India and other postcolonial nations as adapting older forms of empire in new geopolitical clothing? In *The Ministry of Utmost Happiness*, you show us how the Indian government has developed strategies of surveillance and counterterrorism that are, to put it mildly, totalitarian in their scope. How can we think of empire now in the Global South, especially at a time when postcolonial nations are emulating the moral calculus of their old colonial masters?

AR: It is interesting that countries that call themselves democracies—India, Israel, and the United States—are busy running military occupations. Kashmir is one of the deadliest and densest military occupations in the world. India transformed from colony to imperial power virtually overnight. There has not been a day since the British left India in August 1947 that the Indian army and paramilitary have not been deployed within the country's borders against its "own people": Mizoram, Manipur, Nagaland, Assam, Kashmir, Jammu, Hyderabad, Goa, Punjab, Bengal, and now Chhattisgarh, Orissa, Jharkhand. The dead number in the tens or perhaps hundreds of thousands. Who are these dangerous citizens who need to be held down with military might? They are indigenous people, Christians, Muslims, Sikhs, communists. The pattern that emerges is telling. What it shows quite clearly is an "upper"-caste Hindu state that views everyone else as an enemy. There are many who see Hinduism itself as a form of colonialism—the rule of Aryans over Dravidians and other indigenous peoples whose histories have been erased and whose deposed rulers have been turned into the vanquished demons and asuras of Hindu mythology. The stories of these battles continue to live on in hundreds of folktales and local village festivals in which Hinduism's "demons" are other peoples' deities. That is why I am uncomfortable with the word *postcolonialism*.

as: Talk of dissent and social justice has become mainstream in the age of Trump—but social media hashtags often stand in for direct action, and corporations frequently use the language of uplift and social responsibility while doubling down on unethical business practices. Has protest been evacuated of its potential today? And in such an environment, what kind of dissent is capable of cracking the edifice of empire?

ar: You are right. Corporations are hosting happiness fairs and dissent seminars and sponsoring literature festivals in which free speech is stoutly defended by great writers. Dissent Is the Cool (and Corporate) New Way To Be. What can we do about that? When you think about the grandeur of the civil rights movement in the United States, the anti–Vietnam War protests, it makes you wonder whether real protest is even possible any more. It is. It surely is. I was in Gothenburg, Sweden, recently, when the largest Nazi march since World War II took place. The Nazis were outnumbered by anti-Nazi demonstrators, including the ferocious Antifa, by more than ten to one. In Kashmir, unarmed villagers face down army bullets. In Bastar, in Central India, the armed struggle by the poorest people in the world has stopped some of the richest corporations in their tracks. It is important to salute people's victories, even if they don't always get reported on TV. At least the ones we know about. Making people feel helpless, powerless, and hopeless is part of the propaganda.

But what is going on in the world right now is coming from every direction and has already gone too far. It has to stop. But how? I don't have any cure-all advice, really. I think we all need to become seriously mutinous. I think, at some point, the situation will become unsustainable for the powers that be. The tipping point will come. An attack on Iran, for example, might be that moment. It would lead to unthinkable chaos, and out of it something unpredictable would arise. The great danger is that, time and time again, the storm of rage that builds up gets defused and coopted into yet another election campaign. We fool ourselves into believing that the change we want will come with fresh elections and a new president or prime minister at the helm of the same old system. Of course, it is important to bounce the old bastards out of office and bounce new ones in, but that can't be the only bucket into which we pour our passion. Frankly, as long as we continue to view the planet as an endless "resource," as long as we uphold the rights of individuals and corporations to amass infinite wealth while others go hungry, as long as we continue to believe that governments do not have the responsibility to feed, clothe, house, and educate everyone—all our talk is mere posturing. Why do these simple things scare people so much? It is just common decency. Let's face it: the free market is not free, and it doesn't give a shit about justice or equality.

AS: The vexed question of violent struggle against domination has come up at different moments in history. It has been debated in the context of Frantz Fanon's writing, Gandhi, Black Lives Matter, Palestine, and the Naxalite movement, to name a few. It is a question that also comes up in your fiction and nonfiction. What do you make of the injunction against the use of violence in resistance from below?

AR: I am against unctuous injunctions and prescriptions from above to resistance from below. That's ridiculous, isn't it? Oppressors telling the oppressed how they would *like* to be resisted? Fighting people will choose their own weapons. For me, the question of armed struggle versus passive resistance is a tactical one, not an ideological one. For example, how do indigenous people who live deep inside the forest passively resist armed vigilantes and thousands of paramilitary forces who surround their villages at night and burn them to the ground? Passive resistance is political theater. It requires a sympathetic audience. There isn't one inside the forest. And how do starving people go on a hunger strike?

In certain situations, preaching nonviolence can be a kind of violence. Also, it is the kind of terminology that dovetails beautifully with the "human rights" discourse in which, from an exalted position of faux neutrality, politics, morality, and justice can be airbrushed out of the picture, all parties can be declared human rights offenders, and the status quo can be maintained.

AS: While this volume is called *Evil Empire*, a term borrowed from Ronald Reagan's description of the Soviet Union, there are many who think of empire as the only sustainable administrative and political mechanism to manage large populations. How might we challenge dominant voices, such as Niall Ferguson, who put so much faith in thinking with the grain of empire? On the flipside, how might we speak to liberals who put their faith in American empire's militarism in a post–9/11 era? Do you see any way out of the current grip of imperial thinking?

AR: The "managed populations" don't necessarily think from Ferguson's managerial perspective. What the managers see as stability, the managed see as violence upon themselves. It is not stability that underpins empire. It is violence. And I don't just mean wars in which humans fight humans. I also mean the psychotic violence against our dying planet.

I don't believe that the current supporters of empire are supporters of empire in general. They support the *American* empire. In truth, capitalism is the new empire. Capitalism run by white capitalists. Perhaps a Chinese empire or an Iranian empire or an African empire would not inspire the same warm feelings? "Imperial thinking," as you call it, arises in the hearts of those who are happy to benefit from it. It is resisted by those who are not. And those who do not wish to be.

Empire is not just an idea. It is a kind of momentum. An impetus to dominate that contains within its circuitry the inevitability of overreach and self-destruction. When the tide changes, and a new empire rises, the managers will change, too. As will the rhetoric of the old managers. And then we will have new managers, with new rhetoric. And there will be new populations who rise up and refuse to be managed.

What White Supremacists Know

Roxanne Dunbar-Ortiz

THE UNITED STATES has been at war every day since its founding, often covertly and often in several parts of the world at once. As ghastly as that sentence is, it still does not capture the full picture. Indeed, *prior* to its founding, what would become the United States was engaged—as it would continue to be for more than a century following—in internal warfare to piece together its continental territory. Even during the Civil War, both the Union and Confederate armies continued to war against the nations of the Diné and Apache, the Cheyenne and the Dakota, inflicting hideous massacres upon civilians and forcing their relocations. Yet when considering the history of U.S. imperialism and militarism, few historians trace their genesis to this period of internal empire-building. They should. The origin of the United States in settler colonialism—as an empire born from the violent acquisition of indigenous lands and the ruthless devaluation of indigenous lives—lends the country unique characteristics that matter when considering questions of how to unhitch its future from its violent DNA.

The United States is not exceptional in the amount of violence or bloodshed when compared to colonial conquests in Africa, Asia, the

Caribbean, and South America. Elimination of the native is implicit in settler colonialism and colonial projects in which large swaths of land and workforces are sought for commercial exploitation. Extreme violence against noncombatants was a defining characteristic of all European colonialism, often with genocidal results.

Rather, what distinguishes the United States is the triumphal mythology attached to that violence and its political uses, even to this day. The post–9/11 external *and* internal U.S. war against Muslims-as-"barbarians" finds its prefiguration in the "savage wars" of the American colonies and the early U.S. state against Native Americans. And when there were, in effect, no Native Americans left to fight, the practice of "savage wars" remained. In the twentieth century, well before the War on Terror, the United States carried out large-scale warfare in the Philippines, Europe, Korea, and Vietnam; prolonged invasions and occupations in Cuba, Nicaragua, Haiti, and the Dominican Republic; and counterinsurgencies in Columbia and Southern Africa. In all instances, the United States has perceived itself to be pitted in war against savage forces.

Appropriating the land from its stewards was racialized war from the first British settlement in Jamestown, pitting "civilization" against "savagery." Through this pursuit, the U.S. military gained its unique character as a force with mastery in "irregular" warfare. In spite of this, most military historians pay little attention to the so-called Indian Wars from 1607 to 1890, as well as the 1846–48 invasion and occupation of Mexico. Yet it was during the nearly two centuries of British colonization of North America that generations of settlers gained experience as "Indian fighters" outside any organized military institution. While large, highly regimented "regular" armies fought over geopolitical goals in Europe, Anglo settlers in North America waged deadly irregular warfare against the continent's indigenous nations to seize their land, resources, and roads, driving them westward and eventually forcibly relocating them west of the Mississippi. Even following the founding of the professional U.S. Army in the 1810s, irregular warfare was the method of the U.S. conquest of the Ohio Valley, Great Lakes, Southeast, and Mississippi Valley regions, then west of the Mississippi to the Pacific, including taking half of Mexico. Since that time, irregular methods have been used in tandem with operations of regular armed forces and are, perhaps, what most marks U.S. armed forces as different from other armies of global powers.

By the presidency of Andrew Jackson (1829–37), whose lust for displacing and killing Native Americans was unparalleled, the character of the U.S. armed forces had come, in the national imaginary, to be deeply entangled with the mystique of indigenous nations—as though, in adopting the practices of irregular warfare, U.S. soldiers had become the very thing they were fighting. This persona involved a certain identification with the Native enemy, marking the settler as Native American rather than European. This was part of the sleight of hand by which U.S. Americans came to genuinely believe that they had a rightful claim to the continent: they had fought for it and "become" its indigenous inhabitants.

Irregular military techniques that were perfected while expropriating Native American lands were then applied to fighting the Mexican Republic. At the time of its independence from Spain in 1821, the territory of Mexico included what is now the states of California, New Mexico, Arizona, Colorado, Nevada, Utah, and Texas. Upon independence, Mexico continued the practice of allowing non-Mexicans to acquire large swaths of land for development under land grants, with the assumption that this would also mean the welcome eradication of indigenous peoples. By 1836 nearly 40,000 Americans, nearly all slavers (and not counting the enslaved), had moved to Mexican Texas. Their ranger militias were a part of the settlement, and in 1835 became formally institutionalized as the Texas Rangers. Their principal state-sponsored task was the eradication of the Comanche nation and all other Native peoples in Texas. Mounted and armed with the new killing machine, the five-shot Colt Paterson revolver, they did so with dedicated precision.

Having perfected their art in counterinsurgency operations against Comanches and other Native communities, the Texas Rangers went on to play a significant role in the U.S. invasion of Mexico. As seasoned counterinsurgents, they guided U.S. Army forces deep into Mexico, engaging in the Battle of Monterrey. Rangers also accompanied General Winfield Scott's army and the Marines by sea, landing in Vera Cruz and mounting a siege of Mexico's main commercial port city. They then marched on, leaving a path of civilian corpses and destruction, to occupy Mexico City, where the citizens called them Texas Devils. In defeat and under military occupation, Mexico ceded the northern half of its territory to the United States, and Texas became a state in 1845. Soon after, in 1860, Texas seceded, contributing its Rangers to the Confederate cause. After the Civil War, the Texas Rangers picked up where they had left off, pursuing counterinsurgency against both remaining Native communities and resistant Mexicans.

The Marines also trace half of their mythological origins to the invasion of Mexico that nearly completed the continental United States. The opening lyric of the official hymn of the Marine Corps, composed and adopted in 1847, is "From the Halls of Montezuma to the shores of Tripoli." Tripoli refers to the First Barbary War of 1801–5, when the Marines were dispatched to North Africa by President Thomas Jefferson to invade the Berber Nation, shelling the city of Tripoli, taking captives, and blockading key Barbary ports for nearly four years. The "Hall of Montezuma," though, refers to the invasion of Mexico: while the U.S. Army occupied what is now California, Arizona, and New Mexico, the Marines invaded by sea and marched to Mexico City, murdering and torturing civilian resisters along the way.

so what does it matter, for those of us who strive for peace and justice, that the U.S. military had its start in killing indigenous populations, or that U.S. imperialism has its roots in the expropriation of indigenous lands?

It matters because it tells us that the privatization of lands and other forms of human capital are at the core of the U.S. experiment. The militaristic-capitalist powerhouse of the United States derives from real estate (which includes African bodies, as well as appropriated land). It is apt that we once again have a real estate man for president, much like the first president, George Washington, whose fortune came mainly from his success speculating on unceded Indian lands. The U.S. governmental structure is designed to serve private property interests, the primary actors in establishing the United States being slavers and land speculators. That is, the United States was founded as a capitalist empire. This was exceptional in the world and has remained exceptional, though not in a way that benefits humanity. The military was designed to expropriate resources, guarding them against loss, and will continue to do so if left to its own devices under the control of rapacious capitalists.

When extreme white nationalists make themselves visible—as they have for the past decade, and now more than ever with a vocal white nationalist president—they are dismissed as marginal, rather than being understood as the spiritual descendants of the settlers. White supremacists are not wrong when they claim that they understand something about the American Dream that the rest of us do not, though it is nothing to brag about. Indeed, the origins of the United States are consistent with white nationalist ideology. And this is where those of us who wish for peace and justice must start: with full awareness that we are trying to fundamentally change the nature of the country, which will always be extremely difficult work.

The Sources of U.S. Conduct

Stuart Schrader

IMAGINE AN EMPIRE with a massive security sector, one barely accountable to the democratic will. This coercive system, though appearing self-perpetuating, represents an elite echelon's efforts to protect and consolidate power. It employs so many people that its maintenance and funding is necessary, not because of the dictates of national security, but simply to keep all its workers from becoming "superfluous." With a repressive apparatus notorious for its abuses, this security sector fosters the very domestic opposition it is designed to combat.

This outline, to some readers, may sound similar to the military-industrial complex—and its cognate prison-industrial complex—in the United States today. But this description actually comes from George Kennan's foundational article "The Sources of Soviet Conduct," which appeared in *Foreign Affairs*, under the byline X, in 1947. Kennan, perhaps more than anyone else, shaped the rhetoric of the Cold War in a way that made it seem preordained, inevitable. He is most often remembered for calling out the supposedly innate qualities of Russian culture—spiritual deprivation, cynicism, and conformity—upon which communist ideology had been grafted. This combination, he argued, was destined to conflict with the innate qualities of Americanism—its freedom of worship, its emphasis on individuality, and its support of business. But the dominance of the security sector was another persistent motif in Kennan's work; he dedicated five paragraphs of "The Sources of Soviet Conduct" to the "organs of suppression." Secret police lurked everywhere, the narrative went, and prisons were the Soviet Union's primary feature. By 1953, under Joseph Stalin, 2.6 million people were locked up in the gulag and over 3 million more were forcibly resettled— a total of around 3 percent of the population kept under state control. Kennan's point, like those of other foundational Cold War tracts, was clear: unlike the United States, the Soviet Union was brutally repressive.

The idea that fundamental differences in approaches to incarceration drove the conflict between the United States and the Soviet Union strikes an odd chord from the vantage of 2018. Today 2.3 million people are locked up in the United States, and an additional 4.5 million are on parole or probation, for a total of around 2 percent of the population under state control. But while much has been written about how legal changes and racial politics led to the carceral state, it is also helpful to see how Cold War confrontation further contributed to the United States' own gulag.

IN THE SAME YEAR Kennan published as X, the National Security Act created the Department of Defense, the Central Intelligence Agency, and the National Security Council—the building blocks of the national security state. By 1950, in order to further counter the perceived Soviet threat, a top secret but widely known report argued that a blank check for the permanent war economy was needed to establish an offensive global posture. The report, "United States Objectives and Programs for National Security"—better known as NSC 68—planted the vocabulary that became the Cold War's discursive kudzu. Though Kennan himself diverged from its predictions, NSC 68 echoed his formulations, contrasting the importance of U.S. "lawfulness" to Soviet expedience and absolutism.

NSC 68 drew much of its rhetorical power from carceral imagery. "The Soviet monolith," it maintained, "is held together by the iron curtain around it and the iron bars within it, not by any force of natural cohesion." The United States thus had to embark on a massive "build-up of political, economic, and military strength" to take advantage of the Kremlin's "greatest vulnerability," its relationship with the Soviet people. "That relationship," NSC 68 charged, "is characterized by universal suspicion, fear, and denunciation." At its core were "intricately devised mechanisms of coercion" from which the Kremlin's power derived. The report went on to propose that the "artificial mechanisms of unity" of the Soviet police state would crumble if challenged from outside, which is what the cornucopia of U.S. national security spending would do. Though NSC 68 did not make specific recommendations regarding defense expenditures, the Truman administration almost tripled defense spending as a percentage of the gross domestic product between 1950 and 1953 (from 5 to 14.2 percent).

The pathway toward the permanent war economy of NSC 68's vision was not direct. It was contested in Congress and in public opinion. Critics rightly feared the emergence of a "garrison state," a term that has been largely lost today. The necessary shifts entailed liberals accommodating conservatives. As historian Michael J. Hogan detailed, to find a way for fiscal conservatives to accede to the new appropriations that capital-intensive war-making would require in the atomic age, it was necessary for New Dealers to give up hope for continuously robust social-welfare appropriations. After the issuance of NSC 68, debate in Congress over appropriations taught conservatives to "decouple" the national security state "from the economic and social policies of the New Deal," according to Hogan. New tax increases would cover the costs of coercion abroad but not of health, education, and welfare at home. The size of the budget for bombers and submarines would continue to increase, but the size of the social wage would not follow suit. New Dealers pushed "security" to the forefront of the national agenda in the first place by insisting that the government could protect citizens from unpredictable risks; now they were trapped in a cage of their own making.

The result was the military-industrial complex, as Dwight Eisenhower called it in his 1961 farewell speech. He wanted to highlight the entanglement of the military, arms manufacturers, and members of Congress, which he felt was imperiling democratic decision-making over the size of the military, its deployments, and its ever-increasing budget. Eisenhower also worried that a tradition of individual liberty would be difficult to reconcile with a national security state. But while his critique and terminology were indeed useful, Eisenhower was concerned only with the threat from abroad, failing entirely to see what the security state was already accomplishing at home.

From the 1940s through the 1960s, figures in the black freedom struggle—from W. E. B. Du Bois to Jack O'Dell—had been highlighting how the national security state's coercions threatened not just individual freedoms but collective ones. As the United States increasingly accused its own citizens of being subversives, assuming them to be guided by a foreign power, the widely shared images of repression in Soviet society—prisons, exile, staged trials, and the "police apparatus"— became the preeminent security tools to protect the United States against Soviet expansionism. The United States imprisoned communists and black radicals such as Benjamin J. Davis after a series of highly publicized trials. Others, such as Claudia Jones, faced incarceration and then deportation. Reading NSC 68's invocation of prisons and police as the kernel of the vulnerability of the Iron Curtain, then, it is impossible not to sense the paradox of U.S. global leadership. Emily Rosenberg has called it the "central dilemma" of NSC 68: "how to advocate 'freedom' by greatly enlarging the state's capacity for coercion."

THE FEAR OF Soviet expansion and the resulting political instability largely outweighed this philosophical question. One of Eisenhower's own aides, for example, wanted him to emphasize the "worldwide tendency for orderly societies to break down into mob-ridden anarchies." And it was this concern that became the overriding motivation of the Kennedy administration's foreign policy. Not three weeks after Eisenhower's farewell speech, Secretary of State Dean Rusk declared that a "mobile, substantial, and flexible U.S. capability for operations short of general war is essential." Eisenhower adversary General Maxwell Taylor urged Kennedy to adopt this New Frontier policy, which, in practice, meant a focus on "counterinsurgency," with police forces as the "first line of defense" against mob-ridden anarchies around the world, particularly those ginned up by subversives.

The Kennedy administration lodged its new police assistance program in the Agency for International Development, calling it the Office of Public Safety. The program, which was overseen directly by high-ranking National Security Council officials, consolidated and funded what had been a sprawling, poorly resourced, and inefficient set of operations to train, equip, and advise police in Africa, Asia, and Latin America. The goal was to make police in dozens of countries the preeminent tool in the fight against communist subversion. The Office of Public Safety's advisors were experienced law enforcement experts, many of whom spent the immediate aftermath of World War II in the occupations in Germany, Italy, Korea, and Japan. After observing authoritarian police and prison systems firsthand, these experts developed a contrasting commitment to political independence of police and aimed to achieve it through more decentralized organizational reform, technical upgrading, and internal discipline. Their goal was to bolster and educate security forces in "developing countries," and thanks to the constant stream of funding NSC 68 inaugurated, police trainees from other countries quickly learned about "police service under autocratic rule."

But the effort to reject shadowy secret police—and the subversion model that U.S. national security experts feared the Soviets were exporting —was two-faced. The purpose of public safety assistance, advisors insisted, was to enhance democracy. And they aimed to foster respect for constituted authority among the citizenry by making the police efficient and technically adept. As the Office of Public Safety developed and implemented its curriculum, it bequeathed the most modern forms of U.S. policing to the world. Yet with no trace of irony, these lessons detailed how Soviet secret police sent advisors to "vassal" countries to "pull the strings" of the local security apparatus. Moreover, to ensure the mission stayed on course, a number of authoritarian German and Korean officers, especially those known for their exquisite anticommunism, became key U.S. assets in bolstering the security forces in other countries. It was as if the United States thought that to fight creeping authoritarianism, expert authoritarians had to be on hand.

Public safety officers, for example, consistently claimed to teach how *not* to torture suspects during interrogation. And they introduced new counterterrorism techniques. That meant, by Nixon's presidency, showing trainees how improvised bombs were built—to demonstrate, they claimed, how to disarm them. But in both these examples, techniques of repression could easily be reverse-engineered. Many of these aid-recipient countries—from Uruguay to the Philippines—went on to practice harsh forms of policing while paramilitary death squads emerged in others, such as Guatemala. The U.S. image of Soviet repression was mirrored in U.S. client states.

TO UNDERSTAND HOW these public safety advisors then advanced punitive modernization and the carceral state at home, we must return again to 1947. At the very moment the National Security Act took effect, another crucial document in the history of U.S. law enforcement emerged. The President's Committee on Civil Rights had been investigating how law enforcement could safeguard civil rights, especially black civil rights, in the United States. The committee's report to President Harry Truman, *To Secure These Rights*, advocated for what Mary Dudziak has labeled "cold war civil rights." It was necessary to ameliorate racial inequality, this argument went, because the Soviet Union frequently invoked lynching and racial abuses to highlight U.S. hypocrisy.

Although the committee was unflinching in its assessment of how the fundamental civil right to the safety of one's person had been violated frequently (Japanese, Mexicans, and African Americans, as well as members of minority religions, suffered the most), it also understood these problems of racial injustice to be the effect of white extrajudicial violence and "arbitrary" individual actions by cops, particularly in the South. Its solutions were thus focused on strengthening law enforcement and assuring its adherence to due process and administrative fairness. Similar to Kennan, the committee (and the generation of reformers it influenced) believed it was possible to use the tools of policing and prisons fairly, unlike in the Soviet Union.

Political scientist Naomi Murakawa has shown, however, that by framing the problem as arbitrary and as growing out of lawlessness, the committee effectively ruled out the systematic and legally enshrined character of racial abuse. What made it predictable, rather than arbitrary, was its consistent object: racially subjugated peoples. By diminishing the structural aspects of the abuse of minorities, liberal law enforcement reformers opened the door to a wider misunderstanding of what needed to be reformed. The response the committee endorsed—to enact procedural reforms and modernize law enforcement in the United States—rode the high tide of police professionalization initiatives that would crest in the following decades, and which called for a well-endowed, federally sanctioned anticrime apparatus. As historian Elizabeth Hinton and Murakawa have argued, this effort to reform law enforcement and codify its procedures actually made it more institutionally robust and less forgiving, contributing to the country's march toward mass incarceration.

What is less understood, however, is the fundamental mismatch between what reformers and police chiefs imagined reform to look like. For liberal reformers, injustice looked like a lynch mob. For many police experts, steeped in Cold War ideology and trained in counterintelligence, it looked like the Soviet secret police. Mob rule had to be avoided, but so too did centralized authority over police objectives. Underlying reasons for what police did daily, and to whom, was not the concern of either party.

Command-level cops across the United States, after all, were quick to absorb the lessons and perspectives of public safety officers. In policing's professional literatures, CIA officials published articles on topics such as policing in the Soviet Union, which emphasized the centralized governing hierarchy. The fact that Soviet police at the lowest level enacted the tyranny ordered at the top resonated with a generation of U.S. police reformers who had watched corrupt political machines in U.S. cities be dismantled. Police reformers thus demanded that police answer primarily to their own professional guidelines, free from political interference. In this way, the negative model of the authoritarian state was misleading: it may have prevented centralized dictatorial rule, but it left police power largely insulated. And so Cold War U.S. empire abroad found its replica in the War on Crime at home: to break the political syzygy of an authoritarian state apparatus in Sacramento or Saigon, in Wichita or Tokyo, police needed to be technically adept, flush with cash, and insulated from political machinations.

This cohered in the mid-1960s as rioting in U.S. cities and towns caught police underprepared, and officers beat and killed participants and bystanders alike. High-ranking officials in Washington, D.C., and many state capitals turned to the reform experts most familiar with riot control and street protest: public safety advisors. The 1968 anticrime bill thus followed a familiar Cold War model: it funded new federally coordinated riot-control training programs—training that mimicked what the Office of Public Safety urged overseas—and it authorized the purchase of huge supplies of tear gas as well as other technical instruments, from radios to helicopters to tanks.

A revised approach to riot control was but one result of the War on Crime. With a bureaucratic frame of mind that had its closest analog in the military-industrial complex, the "prison-industrial complex" was born out of its zeal for spending on the penal sector. Strategic planning of the best way to utilize those resources fell second. Moreover, by leaning so heavily on Cold War rationales, elected officials and law enforcement leaders started treating criminals as interchangeable with political subversives, thus eschewing rehabilitation efforts, as Micol Seigel has argued. If criminal propensity was similar to the dedication to a cause that marked political radicalism, rehabilitative efforts were pointless.

In 1969 two special investigations concluded that prisons were already ineffective at rehabilitation. New York researchers declared prisons to be hotbeds of radicalism, "more fertile breeding grounds for crime than the streets." Federal research findings, endorsed by James V. Bennett, the retired Federal Bureau of Prisons director, were less caustic but corroborated fears of increasing crime due to the failings of prisons. Bennett was a lifelong reformer; earlier in his career, he had advocated for flexibility in sentencing, educational programs for prisoners, and other hallmarks of rehabilitation. But he and his staff also worked closely with the public safety program, advising prisons in Guatemala and Thailand, and he had spent a few years in occupied Germany learning how to dismantle an authoritarian system. Though Bennett continued to push for educational programs, the final recommendation of his investigation was to dedicate greater resources to incarceration, expand the number of guards, and upgrade the training they received.

The War on Crime was a creature of federalism. Federal appropriations for upgrading police, courts, and prisons came embroidered with a commitment that no usurpation of local authority or discretion would result. Policing remained decentralized. Even when police killed unarmed people during unrest, causing public complaint, police were protected; outrage could be an orchestrated communist plot, the thinking went, intended to take control over law enforcement by undermining its autonomy. In this way, the reform effort preserved the petty despotism of the nightstick and localized tyranny of the police chief that was at the root of the racial crisis. By insulating police from federal oversight or control, while also affording them increased resources, particularly for capital-intensive repressive technologies, the War on Crime allowed the underlying structure of Jim Crow policing to persist.

IN THE END, U.S. police came to see extreme lawfulness—of which they were the sole arbiter—as the rejoinder to Soviet repressiveness, and a vastly inflated penal system as the bureaucratic shield against subversives on U.S. streets. Yet, seeing where it has gotten us—and what we have sacrificed in the process—it is hard not to compare our current system to "organs of suppression." The prison-industrial complex of the present is marked by aggressive and technologically advanced policing, brutal conditions of incarceration, civic exclusion, and fiscal penalties that extends far beyond time served. It has metastasized despite crime declining in the same period. Just as key analysts of the impasse between the Eastern bloc and the United States found that repression seemed to persist for its own sake behind the Iron Curtain, Americans might question the purpose of the contemporary criminal justice system at home.

What made the early Cold War vision of Americanism distinct from that of totalitarianism was that the Soviet police answered directly to political leaders, whereas in the United States police had, by midcentury, mostly thrown off the shackles of the political machine that dictated their terms of employment. This independence remains important for democracy. But as crime continues to decline and appropriations for police continue to grow, the question of democratic control over the instruments of public safety becomes urgent, for public safety appears now to be the instrument for the control of democracy. Law enforcement leaders have become, as Kennan claimed they were in Russia, "masters of those whom they were designed to serve."

Puerto Rico's War on Its Poor

Marisol LeBrón

IN FEBRUARY 1993, war was declared in Puerto Rico. In a special legislative address, Governor Pedro Rosselló pronounced that the time
for half measures was over. The criminals and drug syndicates behind
Puerto Rico's surge in violent crime had "asked for war . . . and war
they will have." In a dramatic step, the governor would be deploying the
National Guard to assist police in drug busts and patrols. This would be
a critical component of his government's new crime-fighting platform,
Mano Dura Contra el Crimen (Iron Fist Against Crime). Although
guardsmen initially patrolled beaches, movie theaters, malls, and other
public spaces, their presence quickly became concentrated in public
housing complexes and other low-income communities.

    Mano Dura, although promoted as a matter of public safety, was
intimately linked with the reengineering of Puerto Rico's public housing
authority. The second-largest under U.S. jurisdiction after New York City's,
the authority had been marked for privatization by the prior administration, ostensibly as a neoliberal experiment in whether homeownership
would combat the "culture of dependency" that had supposedly taken

root there and led to crime and decaying conditions. Naturally, these privatization efforts also held out the promise of lucrative management contracts for well-connected elites. The privatization process was fundamentally undemocratic, and many low-income and black Puerto Ricans rightly felt that *Mano Dura*'s aim of increased safety was simply a front for their dispossession. Further, it soon became abundantly clear that *Mano Dura* was not a panacea for the very serious problems facing public housing residents since, in many cases, it actually worsened the violence and discrimination they faced. Undeterred by resistance from those whom *Mano Dura* was said to help most, the Rosselló administration meanwhile began marketing the campaign as a success in the War on Drugs to be emulated in the United States.

Puerto Rico has had a long history as a laboratory for U.S. domestic and foreign policy. Indeed, the foundation of the contemporary Puerto Rican state—the commonwealth agreement between Puerto Rico and the United States—was conceptualized, in part, as a vehicle to showcase U.S. development strategies to the Third World during the Cold War. Throughout the mid-twentieth century, Puerto Rico was mobilized as an example of the progress that could be achieved through economic and political alignment with the United States.

However, the signing of the North American Free Trade Agreement (NAFTA) in 1992 sounded a death knell for Puerto Rico's special relationship with the United States and threw into question its preferred status as a commonwealth territory. In many ways, this was a tale of a death foretold. As the United States promoted Puerto Rico's development model globally, especially throughout Latin America and Asia, its gradual widespread implementation meant the emergence of new markets and labor pools for U.S. capital beyond the archipelago. As Puerto Rico's economy became more integrated into the U.S. economy—eventually resulting in the extension of federal legal standards and practices, including the federal minimum wage—U.S. capital left the archipelago in search of cheaper labor, better corporate incentives, and less regulation.

In a bid for renewed relevance to the metropole, during the 1990s Puerto Rican elites attempted to reposition Puerto Rico as a model in the arenas of law enforcement and public housing policy, taking it upon themselves to develop new policies and practices regarding security, policing, and public housing policy. For Puerto Rico's governing elite, it was often more important to be seen as "innovative" in the eyes of U.S. technocrats than to implement policies that actually worked. As in the case of *Mano Dura*, this was often accomplished on the backs of some of Puerto Rico's most vulnerable populations.

UNDER *MANO DURA*, approximately eighty-two joint police and military raids—and subsequent occupations—would be carried out in public housing between June 1993 and March 1999. During these raids, police would conduct searches, confiscate contraband, and interrogate residents while the National Guard provided logistical and tactical support in the form of soldiers, helicopters, military vehicles, technology, and weapons. The National Guard was also responsible for setting up surveillance, establishing checkpoints, constructing a perimeter fence around the community, controlling crowds, and detaining suspects that would be taken into police custody. The police and National Guard would then occupy the raided complexes for weeks until a security force of part-time police and private security guards could establish a permanent policing and surveillance presence. This securitization would then provide a stable environment for the management of the complex to be handled by whichever private company had won the bid during a brief process in 1992 that was roundly critiqued at the time for its cronyism and lack of transparency. At its conclusion, the Puerto Rican Housing Authority had awarded contracts to 11 private management firms to deal with the day-to-day maintenance and operation of Puerto Rico's 58,000 public housing units, affecting approximately 60,000 families living in 332 public housing complexes.

Rosselló's use of the National Guard would become one its longest "peacetime" deployments in U.S. history. In 1989 Congress had authorized federal funding to permit National Guard units to support drug interdiction and other counter-drug activities. States desiring to participate in the program were required to draw up plans to be approved by the secretary of defense and Department of Justice. Rosselló was able to skirt some of these requirements by evoking "extraordinary" circumstances to justify the mobilization of military power for the archipelago's war on drugs. Military analysts and strategists therefore watched with curiosity, as Rosselló's repurposing of the Guard seemed to respond to the challenge of what to do with surplus military technology and personnel following the end of the Cold War—a readymade solution to local and federal police agencies looking to be "tough on crime" while adhering to the neoliberal economic imperative to watch their bottom line.

Others took notice as well. *Mano Dura* received coverage in major national news outlets, and, in late 1994, Rosselló was asked to testify before a congressional subcommittee on the use of the National Guard to fight crime. Rosselló encouraged the committee members, "with the Cold War won and the Soviet Union dissolved—the time has come to direct more of our attention to internal security issues; to current dangers we face at home: drug-trafficking, and the violent crime that drug-trafficking engenders." Puerto Rico, Rosselló argued, had "redefined the role of our citizen soldiers" in a way "certainly worthy of study, and maybe emulation." U.S. policymakers, however, struggled with how to reconcile a declared War on Drugs, and the ready availability of surplus military technology and personnel, with the democratic principle of a necessary separation between military and civilian policing.

Indeed, the Clinton administration had already been actively struggling with this question. In late 1993, a year before Rosselló's congressional testimony, Washington, D.C., had sought permission to deploy the National Guard to combat drug-related violence. While nearly fifty guardsmen were already on the streets of the District helping police with drug interdiction efforts, Mayor Sharon Pratt Kelly asked the Clinton administration to make thousands of troops available for up to four months in order to provide tactical support to police during drug enforcement efforts. In a press conference detailing her request in late October 1993, Kelly justified the potential sight of armed soldiers on D.C.'s streets by saying: "We need the Guard's help. We've got a problem that is really of extraordinary proportions. We've got to get real and do whatever it takes to provide safety." Like Rosselló, Kelly appealed to a prevailing sense of panic over "out-of-control" violence.

Four days after Kelly's inquiry, Clinton denied her request. He based his refusal on the fact that guardsmen are not full time and thus an extended mobilization would disrupt their work and family lives. He was also persuaded by a private memo from his counsel that urged him to deny the request on the basis of more substantive concerns about violations of the Posse Comitatus Act, not to mention horrible optics: "Whatever the general authority, the symbolic significance of the President calling out the military to patrol on a regular basis in the shadow of the White House and the Capitol would be enormous." Harold Brazil, a member of the D.C. City Council, put it more bluntly when he told reporters from *Reuters* that he opposed Kelly's request on the grounds that it "would show the world that America's capital is no better than the unstable capital of some anarchist, Third World nation."

The conceptual and physical distancing of Puerto Rico from the United States allowed for the perception that these violations of democratic principles were not already occurring under the U.S. flag and were only possible in the supposedly retrograde space of the Third World.

WHILE IT WAS the initial violent interventions associated with *Mano Dura*—the "Rescue" stage, in official parlance—that often grabbed headlines, the ensuing privatization of Puerto Rico's public housing under military occupation was ultimately of equal interest to U.S. technocrats. In many ways, privatization was always imagined as a desired outcome of *Mano Dura*'s efforts to "cleanse" public housing of drug use and trafficking. Rosa Villalonga, manager of HUD's Caribbean Office, referred to the early morning sieges on public housing as providing a glimpse at "the light at the end of the tunnel" for the long-term goal of privatizing public housing. For Puerto Rican technocrats, *Mano Dura* was understood to be the muscle necessary for privatization to succeed.

Obviously, it was not possible to justify privatization in such explicit terms. Instead, the official narrative played upon familiar tropes of a culture of poverty within low-income communities. Public housing residents' alleged lack of proper work ethic and values were to blame for the precarity that marked their lives. According to housing officials, the dangerous and deteriorating conditions that many public housing residents faced were due to the fact that they had no proprietary claim to their housing units, which contributed to their destructive behaviors. Privatizing public housing and encouraging homeownership among residents would instill residents with a new sense of ownership and pride in their community. There was a catch, however: most residents of public housing had no interest in buying their units. The rents were extremely low compared to market rents or typical mortgage payments, so homeownership offered no clear benefits for many. Further, given the criminalization and discrimination that public housing communities often encountered from their fellow Puerto Ricans, those who could afford to start paying rent or making mortgage payments would prefer to do so elsewhere. Undeterred by a seeming lack of resident buy-in, the Rosselló administration used the militarized conditions enforced by *Mano Dura* to begin privatizing public housing and pushing home-ownership schemes, even if residents had better ideas for how to make their communities safer and foster pride.

Rather than relieving anxiety and fear, military-style occupation coupled with privatization exacerbated dangerous conditions and left residents bereft of input into the governance of their communities. While Rosselló's administration officially celebrated a decrease in the number of robberies and carjackings, Puerto Rico experienced an increase in the murder rate as *Mano Dura* intensified battles between rival gangs over turf. Images of young men lifeless under white sheets haunted the nightly news and provided stark reminders of the intense vulnerability and proximity to violence that many racially and economically marginalized Puerto Ricans continued to experience. Meanwhile growing arrest and incarceration rates fractured families and communities. The number of arrests under Rosselló increased by approximately one-third over that of his predecessor. There were 16,000 arrests recorded in 1992, in contrast to roughly 21,000 arrests in both 1993 and 1994. Under Clinton's federal "one strike and you're out" policy starting in 1996, Puerto Ricans living in public housing faced the additional threat of eviction if they or a family member living with them was convicted of a drug crime. While it seems that the policy was implemented somewhat unevenly in Puerto Rico, doz-ens of Puerto Ricans and their families were evicted. The constant raids in public housing as a result of *Mano Dura* carried not only the threat of incarceration for those swept up in the raids, but also the threat of eviction for their family members, a kind of guilt by association.

Nonetheless, Puerto Rico became a pilgrimage site for U.S. and Latin American policymakers and public officials looking to privatize their own public housing and "modernize" policing in urban areas. These visits to see Puerto Rico's "revolution in public housing" were reminiscent of the trips U.S. and Third World technocrats would take during the 1950s to see Puerto Rico's economic "miracle" following the establishment of the commonwealth arrangement. Visitors included the mayor of New York City, Mario Cuomo; U.S. Drug Czar Lee P. Brown; governmental delegations from Costa Rica and Panama; and officials from the Chicago Housing Authority, the National Center for Housing Management in Washington, D.C., and the Cuban American National Council in Miami.

For their part, Puerto Rican elites went out of their way to make Puerto Rico into a kind of technocratic Disneyland. For example, in 1994 they produced a three-day conference about privatization and securitization that was attended by, among others, representatives from the D.C. Department of Public and Assisted Housing. The conference, hosted at the luxurious Caribe Hilton, was attended by four staff members of the D.C. agency as well as four of its tenants, and was meant to show how the changes taking place in Puerto Rico's public housing could be translated to other public housing authorities around the United States. The conference featured workshops on privatization, crime and drug prevention, and entrepreneurship, in addition to tours of three occupied public housing complexes. According to Anne Clark, chairwoman of the D.C. Resident Council Advisory Board, the conference was generative: "We learned quite a bit. . . . We learned about the different ways that residents are starting their own businesses and that the National Guard carry M-16 rifles to secure public housing properties." While

Clark celebrated resident entrepreneurship, which was supported by private management companies and the Puerto Rico Public Housing Authority, her jarringly matter-of-fact description of soldiers patrolling public housing with assault weapons highlights the ways in which security and profit were intertwined and dependent upon one another.

Puerto Rican officials acknowledged that the success of privatization depended on the intervention of the police and National Guard, but the results, they felt, spoke for themselves: private, independent communities instead of low-income neighborhoods of perpetual renters. This rhetoric greatly exaggerated the gains of Puerto Rico's so-called "experiment in public housing" since, for the most part, only a small number of public housing complexes were actually sold or were slated to be sold by the end of Rosselló's term. In the vast majority of cases, the government privatized only the *management* of the complexes. This rhetoric also denied the experiences of Puerto Rican public housing residents, who voiced concern over the failures of both privatization and militarized policing to make their communities safe or even *theirs*.

ALTHOUGH THE NATIONAL GUARD did not end up being mobilized to secure public housing complexes across the United States, it is nonetheless clear that Puerto Rico was a key player in a conversation taking place during the 1990s that worked to twin privatization and militarized policing as a strategy for urban renewal and public safety. The point of tracing these policy circuits is not that Puerto Rico was the first of its kind, or that these punitive policies and their neoliberal logic were wholly unprecedented. Indeed, *Mano Dura*, despite the rhetoric of innovation, was the progeny of already existing initiatives, policies, and rhetorics, from Broken Windows policing to the ghetto sweeps that made themselves felt in low-income communities of color across the United States long before Rosselló had ever uttered the phrase *Mano Dura Contra el Crimen*. As much as *Mano Dura* served as a policy model, it was also an expression of larger transformations that we now recognize as key components of the neoliberal common sense of our times, under which poor people of color routinely find themselves gentrified and surveilled out of their neighborhoods with the help of police who have been trained and equipped as a domestic military.

As in Los Angeles, Chicago, Ferguson, and other communities ravaged by capital extraction facilitated by the power of a badge, the results in Puerto Rico have been devastating. Public housing residents continue to suffer the wide-ranging effects of systemic discrimination, while the storied public-private partnership that began in the early 1990s—"Puerto Rico's public housing revolution"—has not prevented the physical infrastructure of public housing from falling into various states of neglect and disrepair. Nor has it prevented communities from being displaced through the demolition of "particularly troubled" housing complexes that apparently even privatization could not help. Entire communities disappeared in a cloud of dust and debris, with any sense of ownership and investment that residents had in their homes gone along with it. Corruption scandals plagued the Rosselló administration, and it would go down as one of the most corrupt in Puerto Rico's history. The sweetheart deals, the massive spending on public works projects, and the millions and millions spent on securitizing the Puerto Rican landscape should be scrutinized as we search for the roots of Puerto Rico's debt crisis. But this is also part of the neoliberal order which we are now so primed to expect: the white men at the top collect their pay while people of color at the bottom are left with nothing.

LeBrón

Empire's Racketeers

Pankaj Mishra interviewed by Wajahat Ali

PANKAJ MISHRA DOES NOT suffer fools. Born and raised in North India, the forty-eight-year-old writer was expected to join the civil service after graduating from university; instead he moved to a small village in the Himalayas for five years and wrote literary reviews for the Indian press. In 1995 he published his first book, a travelogue populated by colorful and diverse characters living at the intersection of globalization and Indian tradition. Since then, he has turned out numerous essays, edited an anthology, and published a novel and five books of nonfiction, using his incisive pen to expose the devastating consequences of Western imperialism, globalization, and capitalism.

Five years ago I interviewed Mishra in these pages to discuss his book *From the Ruins of Empire* (2012), which crafted an epic narrative of Middle Eastern and Asian communities seeking empowerment after centuries of European colonization. Mishra has since turned his focus to the origins of modern reactionary forces—from the Islamic State to Brexit and the presidency of Donald Trump. Longlisted for the Orwell Prize, his latest book, *Age of Anger* (2017), seeks to explain why millions feel disenchanted by promises of the progress that was supposed to be delivered by liberal democracy. He traces this phenomenon to the eighteenth and nineteenth centuries, when communities in Africa and Asia were crushed under the imperial wheels of Enlightenment. These ideologies of the elite could not operate, he says, without "intellectual racketeers," the thought leaders who subordinate their intellect and conscience to gain access to power and wealth. Among the current iteration of thought leaders, those now shilling for neoliberalism instead of Enlightenment, he has publicly blasted psychologist and best-selling author Jordan Peterson, whom he accuses of peddling "right-wing pieties seductively mythologized for our current lost generations."

In this exchange, Mishra and I discuss Trump's America First isolationism and its consequences for a rising Asia; the rise of right-wing Hindu nationalism under Indian Prime Minister Narendra Modi; Europe's flirtation with authoritarianism and anti-immigrant hysteria; and the role of the public intellectual in the face of imperial injustice.

WAJAHAT ALI: Trump campaigned on an "America First" platform, vacating the United States' role as a global superpower in order to pursue a nationalist, protectionist, and isolationist vision. China has stepped up to fill the void; it is still committed to the Iran Deal and Paris Agreement and has made heavy investments in Africa and Pakistan, not to mention flexing its muscle in the South China Sea and seeking improved relations with North Korea. Is the axis of power pivoting to a rising China? A well-known filmmaker who lives in South Asia once told me, "Yes, America has its many sins, but at least it has a soul. Imagine what will happen if China or Russia replaces it." And here we are.

PANKAJ MISHRA: I don't think Asians or South Asians have much cause for celebration if power is indeed shifting to the East—if there are now plenty of crazy rich Asians as well as Americans. One has to step away from these simple formulas and ask, *whose* power, *whose* wealth? Who in Asia will these transformations empower or enrich, and what will be the political consequences of deepening inequality in such populous countries? Asians have shown themselves very capable of the same kind of calamitous blunders as those of their former Western overlords. Japan's history of militarism and imperialism should be a warning to all those who look to China; to this day the ghost of nationalism is yet to be exorcised there. And we know about South Asia's inability to defuse its toxic nationalisms or provide a degree of social and economic justice to its billion-plus populations.

I also think we need to question the idea that Trump's America First agenda is unprecedented, that the U.S. imperium—whether under Republicans or Democrats—has not continuously violated international norms. Didn't Barack Obama threaten to renegotiate NAFTA? Didn't George W. Bush put Iran in the "Axis of Evil" and openly scorn France and Germany for failing to join his misadventure in Iraq? It has become too easy since Trump's ascension to say that the United States once advanced liberal democracy and freedom. This was never the view from India or Pakistan, let alone Iran, Iraq, and Afghanistan. The United States was and is a self-interested global hegemon; it has supported the world's worst despots when they seemed to protect U.S. interests. The only difference is that Trump openly repudiates emollient rhetoric and does not hesitate to alienate U.S. allies.

WA: And he is not alone. A string of right-wing leaders—Benjamin Netanyahu, Rodrigo Duterte, Viktor Orbán, Narendra Modi, Recep Tayyip Erdoğan—are still winning democratic elections and retaining popularity despite resorting to authoritarian tactics. In your most recent book, *Age of Anger* (2017), you argue that this troubling trend is the inevitable afterbirth of modern progress. Contrary to Francis Fukuyama's prediction, Western liberal democracies did not herald the "end of history." Instead they seem to have contained within them the seeds of our destruction. Is there any hope for these systems and institutions? Or, in their place, is absolutism—whether from the right or the left—the inevitable result?

PM: As a writer I am more interested in describing the past accurately than in outlining the future; we need a new past if we are to make sense of our intolerable present or work to change it. One of my favorite historians, Carl Becker, wrote that "in periods of stress, when the times are thought to be out of joint, those who are dissatisfied with the present are likely to be dissatisfied with the past also." In that vein, I have been trying to advance a story of the past that helps us understand the deep roots of our global crisis, the present outbreaks of demagoguery—in the heart of the modern West as well as in Asia and Africa, where it had been too easy to blame religion and culture for the failings of postcolonial societies. In the book, I am pushing back against the dominant narrative that presents grotesquely unjust societies, built on violence and dispossession, as the best possible world.

Boosting Western-style democracy and capitalism, and ignoring their long history of complicity with imperialism, the end-of-history narrative has made it too easy to deny the simple fact, as Orwell put it, that "the European peoples, and especially the British, have long owed their high standard of life to direct or indirect exploitation of the coloured peoples." Those of us who grew up in places despoiled by capitalist imperialism—India, Nigeria, China—were left in no doubt by our history textbooks that it brought our world into being and made it what it is. These nationalist histories had their own distortions, but they got some basic things right. Look at the Chinese narrative about the "hundred years of humiliation" or the Declaration of the Independence of India (1929) and you see the same historical outline: how the forces of industrialized production in nineteenth-century Europe and the United States expanded through genocide and slavery, or, at the very minimum, through military invasion, occupation, and dispossession.

The strange thing for me, when I first left India in my mid-twenties and traveled to the West, is how differently people saw this history. Structural and extensive violence had been carefully hidden from its long-term beneficiaries. They saw themselves as the inheritors of wonderfully inventive white people who had mapped the world and created the political and economic possibility of individual freedom for everyone. In truth, these were the paternalistic forms of a harsh theory and practice of domination and supremacy, which presumed to bring civilization to benighted natives.

Supremacy of all stripes—racial, ethnic, national—works in insidious ways, burrowing deep inside impeccably liberal minds. In retrospect it seems a bit unfair of me to single out a figure such as Niall Ferguson for peddling bogus histories of empire, free trade, and democracy: those ideas have long informed much mainstream and respectable journalism. So effective have those narratives been that even the long-term victims of the history of violence have found it hard to build international solidarities. In the latter half of the twentieth century, most Asian, African, and African American thinkers and activists recognized that decolonization and the civil rights movement were part of the same battle—but that essential view has been mostly lost. Writers from historically disadvantaged communities have become more parochial and less internationalist in their thinking. In a recent review I pointed out how even such a sensitive and brilliant writer as Ta-Nehisi Coates could not relate the African American experience to the history of Asia and Africa—and how this failure made him invest too much faith in Barack Obama, a dutiful sentinel of the U.S. imperium.

Of course, self-congratulatory white histories—Plato to NATO via the Reformation, Renaissance, and Enlightenment—are not very persuasive today, and long-suppressed realities have erupted to the surface. We are beginning to understand what anti-imperialists such as Du Bois and Gandhi saw so clearly: white supremacy is the malign force of modern history. With old-style racist imperialism no longer an option, those fearful of the loss of white power look to brute authority figures. These ugly facts tell us that a system so parasitic on violence and dispossession, so prone to generating cruel inequality and inflicting injustice, should not be saved. We need a fresh vision of political and economic possibilities—one that is not derived from the history of capitalist expansion and imperialism.

WA: At the same time that identities are consolidating once again around religion, ethnicity, and nationality, we are also seeing an erasure and reconfiguration of bodies, borders, and boundaries. The sins and ghosts of many Western nations are ending up at the doorstep of Europe, testing the limits of its alleged liberalism. Will Europe be able to reconcile its history of racism, colonialism, and Islamophobia with its refugee crisis?

PM: We have to examine more closely just when and how Europe became an exemplar of liberal democracy—an idea that derives from Europe's wholly exceptional postwar period, when it recovered from a long stint in pure hell. We have all heard of the genocide committed by Germans. But ethnic cleansing was at the foundation of many of Europe's contemporary nation-states. Even during *les Trente Glorieuses* (the thirty "glorious" years between 1945 and 1975), Europe was hardly a global exemplar of liberalism. Spain and Portugal were closer to despotism than democracy until the 1970s; parts of rural Italy, Spain, and Portugal actually looked like the Third World. It is true that by the 1990s the rights of women, factory workers, and sexual minorities were never as secure as in the UK, France, Germany, the Netherlands, and Scandinavia. But Europe never ceased to have problems with accepting people from Asia and Africa, who were brought in to service the new miracle economies. The coming of neoliberalism after the fall of communism only made things worse, spreading a new ideological fervor on behalf of efficiency, flexibility, and marketization. Its devastating effects in Russia in the 1990s already pointed to a new era of oligarchy and messianic politics. Nearly thirty years later, its consequences in Europe—widespread dispossession, destruction of traditional livelihoods, denial of dignity, and compensatory scapegoating of immigrants—are all too clear. Whiteness has reemerged as a virulent political religion, but it is important to remember that large parts of Europe were never really comfortable with racial heterogeneity.

WA: You've been critical of India's engagement with globalization. Modi was elected prime minister in 2014, having run on Hindu nationalism and his pro-business record. Since then India's economy has grown, but there has also been rampant income inequality and a surge in mob violence against minorities, especially Muslims accused of eating beef. In July India's Supreme Court condemned this "mobocracy." How have Modi's economic and political policies, which were supposed to create more open and free societies, been used and manipulated for oppression?

PM: We have to look at what specific processes of globalization amount to in India, rather than accept at face value the ideological claims made for them. There has been a lot of self-congratulation—among both

Indian and Western commentators—about Indian democracy, but none of it can explain a figure such as Modi and why India is more violent today than it was under British rule. To examine these particular experiences is also to begin to learn what kind of politics and economy work best for our complex societies. It is to move away from neo-imperialist visions of Asia, according to which its countries are forever competing in a race to Western-style modernity. Along with U.S. libertarian fantasists, many liberals in India welcomed Modi, seeing him as an economic modernizer and taking for granted the resilience of democracy. For many he was proof of India's democratic revolution. His record of instigating violence against minorities was either ignored or denied. Anyone aware of his background—for example, his lifelong membership in Rashtriya Swayamsevak Sangh, an organization inspired by European fascists—knew what he would do in power: try to forge a Hindu nation by demonizing minorities and left-leaning dissenters. I keep saying this: it is our own ignorance, or denial, of the tragically entwined history of capitalist expansion and democracy that makes us expect benign outcomes from them.

WA: Speaking of Indian democracy, you have written that "the formal and proceduralist features of democracy—elections—have superseded their substantive aspect: strong, accountable, and fair-minded institutions and officials." How can Indians engage the democratic process in a meaningful manner? If this is not possible, then is democracy the best solution for achieving political equality in India?

PM: The answer to the many problems, inadequacies, and dangers of democracy should never be less democracy. It is true that in many parts of the world, ordinary citizens feel disenfranchised by alliances between national politicians and global businessmen. Liberal democracy—with its subordination of such substantive matters as equality, freedom, and general welfare to procedural issues, its obsession with the holding of elections and the preservation of norms—has turned out to be the best way of concentrating and deepening oligarchic power. This is the main reason it has provoked such furiously emphatic rejections worldwide from voters who feel utterly deceived and powerless, who no longer believe that liberal democracy is superior to authoritarian rule.

Still, the answer is not less democracy, or authoritarian populism. We need *more* democracy in India and elsewhere—substantive democracy. It is a truism that democracy in its Western habitat struggled for a long time to concede equal rights to slaves, women, workers, and the colonized on the grounds that they were deficient in reason. The project of equality and freedom was also continuously undermined by the rise of a market economy and a bureaucratic state, which placed economic and political rationality above moral claims. In many ways democracy in its ideal form has been more clearly formulated in postcolonial nations, where it was attached from the very beginning to promises of equality, social and economic justice, and the welfare of the poor and underprivileged castes. We need to rebuild and reinstitutionalize this vision. We say we believe in democracy. But the urgent question, wherever we are, is *what kind of democracy.* One where wage slavery is the norm? Where politicians deploy the ample tools of demagoguery to get elected and then ignore ordinary voters? Or, instead, one in which power is not concentrated at the top and people feel themselves to be citizens as well as voters, able to participate in making decisions that affect their lives? The latter is obviously preferable, but it will be difficult to work our way to it. Political elites have used elections and parliaments as instruments of legitimacy; they exercise monopoly power in the media as well, and they will not give it up easily.

WA: Your critiques of Salman Rushdie and Niall Ferguson have generated considerable notoriety. And you recently wrote a scathing review of Jordan Peterson's best-selling *12 Rules for Life: An Antidote to Chaos,* calling it a brand of "intellectual populism" that is "packaged for people brought up on Buzzfeed listicles," a category that seems predominantly to include young men. You also accused him of romancing the noble savage. He responded by calling you an "arrogant, racist son of a bitch" and threatened to slap you—a threat he reiterated at a conference I recently attended. As a person of color, a South Asian man in particular, do you feel you have a particular role as a public intellectual in challenging academics who find comfort in an order and hierarchy that privileges white men? What should be the role of public intellectuals—especially those of color—today?

PM: I think the fact that we have to ask this question shows how serious the problem has become. Many people we think of as intellectuals—our "thought leaders"—are basically global professionals, adept movers in the networks of Oxbridge, the Ivy League, the London School of Economics, think tanks, Davos, and Aspen. The result, as we see more clearly after Trump, has been a stultifying sameness in the public intellectual sphere: loud echo chambers in which you have a whole class of writers and journalists saying the same things over and over again. This is why our political crisis today is, first and foremost, a global intellectual crisis—the result of a feckless homogenization of thought.

We have had these academic superstars who went on about knowledge and power but were themselves busy climbing social ladders. Even writers and intellectuals with a great deal of integrity and courage have become too professionalized, too career-oriented, and too concerned not to upset their peers—not to mention those they regard as their more famous and successful superiors. This professional docility has allowed figures such as Ferguson to flourish, and that is why criticism drives them to hysteria today.

There is hope, though. It is true that Trump has opened up space for all kinds of intellectual racketeers, who pose as members of an intellectual Maquis while trying to save or advance their professional careers. These dead-end centrists—most of whom moonlighted as laptop bombers during the Iraq War and often advised the Clintons, Blair, Bush, and Obama—still dominate many high-circulation periodicals. They present a huge but neglected problem. You can get rid of incompetent or venal rulers through the democratic process, but there is nothing you can do with the deadweight at the highest editorial levels of mainstream media. These figures who were wrong or clueless about every major domestic and foreign policy issue—from Russia in the 1990s to Iraq and the financial crisis—remain entrenched, starving the public of much-needed fresh ideas and compounding the political calamity of elite centrism with a massive intellectual and moral failure.

But in response, the intellectual culture of the left is flourishing once again after many barren decades—often outside its usual setting of academia, in small magazines and webzines, including these very pages. Many academics—a few names attest to their range: Amia Srinivasan, Adam Tooze, Kate Manne, Samuel Moyn, Aziz Rana, Nancy Maclean, Quinn Slobodian, Jennifer Pitts, Corey Robin—have stepped into the fray with complex yet accessible analyses of the impasse we inhabit today. Bold charlatans such as Jordan Peterson will no doubt induce awe at the *Atlantic*, and Enlightenment-mongers such as Steven Pinker will continue to impress many rich dullards, but they will also be taken to the cleaners by historians and anthropologists.

WA: The *Economist* has labeled you the "heir to Edward Said." How do you respond to the comparison?

PM: Not very well. These kinds of intellectual genealogies are very superficial—sound bites, essentially. The important work of Edward Said—the examination and overcoming of degraded and degrading representations of the non-West—is being carried on by many writers, and it is far from finished. It has suffered serious setbacks in the post–9/11 era, which has seen an exponential rise in bigoted ideas, so we need many more people with his intellectual capacity and moral courage to challenge mainstream prejudices. It is also true that Said represented only one side of the great work undertaken by writers and scholars from the non-Western world; there are many Western and non-Western intellectual traditions and figures I feel much closer to.

And one has to ask why the Anglo-American press feels compelled to make such comparisons. It has been indifferent to, if not contemptuous of, the experiences and perspectives of non-white peoples and invests too much in token gestures to diversity, anointing this or that writer—Rushdie yesterday, Coates and Chimamanda Adichie today, someone else tomorrow—as the representative of a nation, race, and religion. Individual writers must reject such a dubious honor—the burden of singularity—and insist on the great variety and complexity of the experience that their white audience wants them to simplistically embody.

Intellectuals Against Noticing

Jeanne Morefield

AFTER TWO YEARS of President Donald Trump, critics and commentators are still struggling to make sense of his foreign policy. Despite some hopes that he might mature into the role of commander in chief, he has continued to thumb his nose at most mainstream academic frameworks for analyzing and conducting foreign policy. Indeed, what makes Trump's interactions with the rest of the world so confusing is the way he flirts with, and then departs from, the script. He may issue policies and give speeches that include words such as "sovereignty," "principled realism," and "peace through strength," but they frequently appear cheek by jowl with racist rants, crass opportunism, nationalist tirades, and unrestrained militarism.

It is this uncomfortable mixture of familiar and jarring that has proven disconcerting for many mainstream international relations scholars, particularly those "intellectual middlemen" who straddle the realms of academia, policy think tanks, and major news outlets. Yet rather than ask how U.S. foreign policy might have contributed to the global environment that made Trump's election possible, most have responded to the inconsistencies of Trump's world vision by emphasizing its departure from everything that came before and demanding a return to more familiar times. International relations experts thus express nostalgia for either the "U.S.-led liberal order" or the Cold War while, in outlets such as *Foreign Affairs* and the *New York Times*, they offer selective retellings of the country's past foreign policies that make them look both shinier and clearer than they were. These responses do not offer much insight into Trump himself, but they do have much to tell us about the discourse of international relations in the United States today and the way its mainstream public analysts—liberals and realists alike—continue to disavow U.S. imperialism.

For example, liberal internationalists such as John Ikenberry argue that Trump is guilty of endangering the U.S.-led global order. That system, according to Ikenberry and Daniel Deudney, emerged after World War II, when the liberal democracies of the world "joined together to create an international order that reflected their shared interests," while simultaneously agreeing, as Ikenberry once put it, to transfer "the reins of power to Washington, just as Hobbes's individuals . . . voluntarily construct and hand over power to the Leviathan." The vision of cooperating nation-states may have originated in values that first "emerged in the West," they argue, but these values have since "become universal." In this accounting, Trump threatens the stability of U.S. liberal hegemony in two ways: by retreating from multilateral agreements such as the Iran nuclear deal, and by refusing to participate in the narrative of enlightened U.S. leadership. Future great threats to global stability, Ikenberry grumbled, were supposed to come from "hostile revisionist powers seeking to overturn the postwar order." Now a hostile revisionist power "sits in the Oval Office."

By contrast, when realists such as Stephen Walt or John Mearsheimer criticize Trump, they start from the position that the liberal world order is a delusion, perpetuated most recently by post–Cold War members of the "elite foreign policy establishment." Walt and others rightly point to the baseline hypocrisy of a "liberal Leviathan," noting that the current fury over Russian election tampering and cyber espionage rings hollow given the long U.S. reliance on both strategies. This view accompanies a wistful longing for the putatively gimlet-eyed realism of the Cold War, a time when U.S. presidents understood that their role was to deter the Soviet Union, prevent the emergence of dangerous regional hegemons, and preserve "a global balance of power that enhanced American security." Seen thus, Trump's hyperbolic and embarrassing nationalism is a symptom of the abandonment of great power politics, while his fawning treatment of Vladimir Putin shatters any remaining hope that his self-styled "principled realism" might take us back to a more strategically realistic time. In the words of former Secretary of Defense Ash Carter, watching the Trump–Putin news conference was like "watching the destruction of a cathedral."

But what is Trump actually doing to destroy this cathedral? What makes Trump's words and behavior so objectionable? Previous presidents have pulled out of multilateral agreements, entered into disputes with allies, and engaged in protectionism and trade wars. The majority of the Trump administration's planned and ongoing military deployments are in regions where the military was already deployed by previous administrations in the name of the War on Terror. Moreover, Trump's national security and national policy statements are littered with the vocabulary of the very experts who find him so terrifying. What, then, makes Trump's foreign policy such a singular threat?

Trump's foreign policy is disturbing because it is uncanny—both grotesque *and* deeply familiar. Like a funhouse mirror, Trump's vision of the world reflects back a twisted image of U.S. global politics that *is* and *is not* who we are supposed to be. For instance, deterrence strategy may require the rest of the world to believe that the U.S. president might use nuclear weapons, but the president is *not* supposed to hint that he might actually do so. The president is supposed to be concerned with regulating the flow of immigrants but *not* reveal that race plays a role in these calculations by blurting the phrase "shithole countries." The president is supposed to believe that the United States is the most blessed, exceptional country on Earth—as Barack Obama put it, "I believe in American exceptionalism with every fiber of my being"—but *not* engage in excessive nationalism by making "total allegiance" the "bedrock" of his politics, or combine it with a commitment to "make our Military so big, powerful & strong that no one will mess with us."

Sometimes Trump's utterances hit so close to home that they surpass uncanniness. In an essay by Sigmund Freud on the uncanny, Freud says dolls and mannequins unsettle precisely because of the possibility that they might actually be alive, a discomfort that has inspired nightmares, works of literature, and horror movies. Trump, by contrast, is a living nightmare. He opens his mouth and the things-which-must-never-be-said simply fall out. Thus, when Bill O'Reilly asked him why he supported Putin even though he is a "killer," Trump shot back, "There are a lot of killers. You think our country's so innocent?"

Trump's willingness to say such things has precipitated an existential crisis in the international relations world. U.S. foreign policy, as an academic discourse and political practice, is built on the delicate foundation of what Robert Vitalis has called the "norm against noticing." This deflective move has long been the gold standard of international relations; under its rules of play, IR experts act as if the United States has never been an imperial power and that its foreign policy is not, and has never been, intentionally racist. The norm against noticing thus distinguishes between the idea of the United States as a necessary world-historical actor and the reality of how the United States acts.

In that reality, the United States has long been an imperial power with white nationalist aspirations. Given the racialized nature of U.S. imperial expansion, it makes sense that Alexis de Tocqueville predicted, in a chapter entitled "The Three Races of the United States," that the United States would one day govern "the destinies of half the globe." In its early days, while still a slave-holding country, the United States asserted its sovereignty through genocide on a continental scale and annexed large portions of northern Mexico. The country went on to overthrow the independent state of Hawaii, occupied the Philippines and Haiti, exerted its regional power throughout Latin America, expanded its international hegemony after World War II, and became what it is today: the world's foremost military and nuclear power with a $716 billion "defense" budget that exceeds the spending of all other major global powers combined.

"Taking over from the British Empire in the early twentieth-century," argues James Tully, the United States has used its many military bases located "outside its own borders"—now nearly 800 in over 80 countries—to force open-door economic policies and antidemocratic regimes on states throughout the formerly colonized world. An extremely partial list of sovereign governments that the United States either overthrew or attempted to subvert through military means, assassinations, or election tampering since 1949 includes Syria, Iran, Guatemala, Lebanon, the Congo, Cuba, Chile, Afghanistan, Nicaragua, Grenada, Cuba, Korea, Vietnam, Cambodia, Iraq, Yemen, Australia, Greece, Bolivia, and Angola. Such interventionist policies have contributed substantially to today's inegalitarian world in which an estimated 783 million people live in profound poverty. In sum, for untold millions of humans in the Global South, the seventy years of worldwide order, security, and prosperity that Ikenberry and Deudney associate with Pax Americana has been anything but ordered, secure, or prosperous.

And yet the norm against noticing prevents foreign policy analysis from even acknowledging—let alone grappling with—the relationship between race and imperialism that has characterized U.S. international relations from the country's earliest days. This regime of politely unseeing—of deflecting—connections between U.S. foreign policy, race hierarchy, and colonial administration was clearly not in effect when *Foreign Affairs* was released under its original name: the *Journal of Race Development*. This began to change, however, in the 1920s. Among other contributing factors, World War I, the rise of anti-colonial revolutions, and the emergence of liberal internationalism as a popular ideology helped convince foreign policy experts in the United States and Europe to adopt a policy language oriented toward "development" rather than imperialism or racial difference. Mainstream international relations scholarship today remains committed to a narrative in which the discipline itself and U.S. foreign policy has always been and remains race blind, concerned solely with the relationship between sovereign states who cooperate, deter, or compete with one another in a global system in which the United States is simply, like Caesar, the "first citizen" (Ikenberry) or "the luckiest great power in modern history" (Walt). For liberals, this involves a studied erasure of the imperial origins of twentieth-century internationalism in the League of Nations' Mandate system and the complicity of Woodrow Wilson in preserving, as Adom Getachew puts it, "white supremacy on a global scale." For realists, it requires both forgetting the anti-Enlightenment origins of postwar realist thought and reinserting the "security dilemma" back into history so that, with the help of Thucydides, Machiavelli, and Hobbes, the world can—as Slavoj Žižek says—"become what it always was."

International relations experts will acknowledge U.S. violence and overreach when necessary, but routinely read the illiberalism of U.S. foreign policy as an exception that is not at all representative, in Anne Marie

Slaughter's words, of "the idea that is America." Slaughter, with Ikenberry, can consider bad behavior only briefly and only in the service of insisting that what matters most is not what the United States actually *does* with its power but what it *intends* to do. Yes, "imperialism, slavery, and racism have marred Western history," Ikenberry and Deudney argue, but what matters is that liberalism "has always been at the forefront of efforts—both peaceful and militant—to reform and end these practices." Indeed, even those public intellectuals such as Niall Ferguson and Michael Ignatieff who, after September 11, called for the United States to *embrace* its status as an imperial power, framed their arguments in deflective, liberal terms. By contrast, because realists project the security dilemma retroactively into history (while also simultaneously excising imperialism) they can only see the U.S. destabilization of Third World economies, assassinations, and secret bombings as tragic necessities (great powers, claims Mearsheimer, "have little choice but to pursue power and to seek to dominate the other states in the system") or as the result of liberals' ill-advised desire to force "our" values on other nations. Both of these deflective strategies reinforce the illusion that we live, in Nikhil Pal Singh's words, in an "American-centered, racially inclusive world, one organized around formally equal and independent nation states" where some states just happen to have more power than others, and where the alternative—Russian or Chinese hegemony—is too frightening even to contemplate.

That deflection would play such an outsized role in supporting the ideological edifice of international relations today is hardly surprising. Turn-of-the-century British liberals who supported their empire also drew upon a variety of different deflective strategies to reconcile the violence and illiberalism of British imperial expansion with the stated liberal goals of the Empire. Such deflection made it impossible for these thinkers—many of whom would go on to work as some of the first international relations scholars in Britain and help found The Royal

Institute of International Affairs—to link the problems of empire with the violence and disruption of imperialism.

Similarly, deflection within international relations today obscures the U.S. role in maintaining the profoundly hierarchical, racist, insecure, deeply unjust reality of the current global order. It also makes it impossible to address how U.S. foreign policy (covert and overt) has contributed to the destabilization of that order by creating the circumstances that give rise to "failed states," "rogue regimes," and "sponsors of terrorism." Moreover, it impedes any theorizing about how the widespread appeal of Trump's xenophobia at home might, in part, be the product of U.S. foreign policy abroad, the bitter fruit of the War on Terror and its equally violent predecessors. In other words, in the grand tradition of liberal empire, U.S. foreign policy deflection actively disrupts the link between cause and effect that an entire science of international relations was created to explain.

WHAT MAKES TRUMP'S ATTITUDE toward foreign policy so uniquely unhinging for international relations experts, then, is the fact that it is essentially undeflectable. When he explains to Theresa May that refugees threaten European culture or calls Mexican immigrants killers, he lays bare the meant-to-be unutterable fear of nonwhite migration that has haunted British, U.S., and European imperialists and foreign policy experts for over a century. When he summons the fires of nationalism to demand an unprecedented increase in the military budget, and then gets it with the overwhelming support of House and Senate Democrats, he reveals that constitutional checks on the commander in chief are only as good as the willingness of Congress to resist jingoism. When he calls nations populated by brown and black people shitholes, he openly advertises the unspoken white supremacist edge that has informed U.S. economic, development, energy, and foreign policies since the late nineteenth century. Trump's Muslim ban is simply the War on Terror on steroids. In short, Trump's foreign policy is unprecedented not because of what it *does*, but because Trump will openly *say* what it does—and because of what that then says about us as a nation.

The discomfort Trump provokes ought to prompt international relations experts to reflect on the failings of their discipline to reckon with the relationship between U.S. imperialism, U.S. foreign policy, and the constellation of xenophobia, militarism, racism, and nationalism that haunts our days. The fields of intellectual and legal history and political theory are far ahead of international relations in their critical interrogation of the ideologies that sustain empire at home and abroad. In addition, Trump's election has emboldened activists to make increasingly explicit the connections they see between a racialized, anti-immigrant politics of domestic dispossession and violence and the history of U.S. imperialism in the world. Unfortunately the same does not appear to be true for the majority of intellectual middlemen who set the public tone for U.S. foreign policy.

Trump is, finally, both the emperor with no clothes and the pointing child, begging to hold a big military parade so we can collectively acknowledge the naked imperialist power at the heart of U.S. foreign policy. Trump practically screams at the United States to look at itself. And yet, the more he screams, the more the intellectual enablers avert their eyes. They are busy looking elsewhere—anywhere really—*except* at that nakedness.

The Burden of Being Good

Michael Kimmage

WHEN RONALD REAGAN described the Soviet Union as an evil empire in his 1983 speech to the National Association of Evangelicals, the empire part was not the sticking point. The United States had often worked with European empires, after all, and Reagan himself had been knighted by Queen Elizabeth II—an accolade, among other things, of the British Empire. For Reagan and many other U.S. presidents, empire was more a fact of life than a self-evident example of politics gone awry. It was the Soviet Union's evil that bothered Reagan. He loathed the Soviet capacity to project that evil through its dominion over others.

And Reagan was right. A thread of evil ran through Soviet history. The Bolsheviks admitted no law higher than their party's expedience as defined by Lenin and Stalin. They imprisoned and executed and tortured at will. They subordinated whole peoples to the state they were building. Siberia's gulag and Moscow's Lubyanka prison were the proof, and they were the tip of the iceberg. Stalin made terror a fulcrum of Soviet society, adding a string of atrocities and secret-police actions in central Europe to his resume.

The Soviet Union moderated after Stalin's death in 1953, but it was an exceptionally coercive state at the best of times—a tyranny and an empire hidden behind the veil of a benevolent and acutely theoretical Marxism–Leninism. Reagan saw evil in the unfreedom of a command economy that left people poor, their potential unrealized, and their creativity eviscerated.

Reagan may have worried most of all about the Soviet Union's refusal to allow religion. "Let us pray," Reagan said in his 1983 "evil empire" speech to the evangelicals—"for the salvation of all of those who live in that totalitarian darkness—pray they will discover the joy of knowing God." What the evangelicals heard, and what they were supposed to hear, was a condemnation of state-imposed atheism in the Soviet Union. While the British Empire housed the Church of England, the Soviet empire housed the perverse relics of Lenin for pilgrims to visit on Red Square. The evil of the Soviet Union, according to Reagan, was its pharaonic contempt for the People of the Book whose sorrow it was to live there.

Yet Reagan was also wrong. The implications of his political metaphysics—the simplified Old Testament flourish that had come so naturally to him—went on to have a corrupting effect on the United States. Reagan made a medieval knight of Washington, placed this knight at the head of a crusade, and waved the banner of righteousness before going on to slay the dragon of evil. Such blissful self-mythologizing incurred two separate costs for U.S. foreign policy vis-à-vis what would become the former Soviet Union. First, it obscured the myriad attachments that Russians (and others) had to their Soviet pasts, rendering aspects of post-Soviet Russian politics incomprehensible. And, second, it made the presumption of goodness continuous with the project of a whole, free, and peaceful Europe. So virtuous was U.S. policy, in Americans' eyes, that there was no one entitled or likely to challenge it until Russia inexplicably did in Georgia in 2008 and then more ambitiously again in Ukraine in 2014. Russia was not just intransigent. Its intransigence was entirely unanticipated in Washington in 2014.

THE UNITED STATES was also operating under a bad analogy. When the Nazi evil empire fell, West Germany exited the forest of its authoritarian history and, by atoning for Hitler's evils, it guaranteed the integrity of German democracy. The German precedent furnished an appealing— even optimistic—course of action for the United States. If the Soviet Union was evil, the story went, it deserved to collapse. It deserved to be replaced by another political system and to be integrated into another international order. And, if the United States was good, it could generously offer to Russia its political system and its idea of international order, once the Soviet Union had finally vanished.

For a while, in the 1990s, it seemed like the familiar script was playing out. Russia acquired a president, it adopted elements of U.S.–style campaigning (Boris Yeltsin famously did a version of the twist on the campaign trail), and capitalism was seemingly the only option. The Russian economy would be subjected to shock therapy as a path to creating a democratic culture. The citizen could vote, the citizen could start a business, and in the public sphere, the citizen could take an honest look at the Soviet past. With knowledge of the crimes and of the evils in the Soviet story, responsibility would surely come. The freedom to know, Germany had already proven, is the freedom to atone.

But the Soviets were not the Nazis. The Soviet Union lost the Cold War by ceasing to exist, but it lost nothing on the battlefield, and post-Soviet Russia was never occupied or reeducated by the United States. The Soviet Union had also existed for far longer than Nazi

Germany had. It had more benign and more pathological phases, the later decades reflecting a steady softening since Stalin's death in 1953. Most importantly, the Nazi analogy broke down because the Soviet Union itself was attacked in 1941. It bore the brunt of Nazi brutality, enduring the worst of the war, and contributing more than any other country to Hitler's defeat. Many Russians today cannot associate their Soviet past with evil primarily because of the Great Patriotic War, their great victory against evil. The contradiction of Stalin's rule was—and remains—formidable for those with a family connection to it. The tyrant who killed with the same abandon Hitler did is also the man who defended the homeland from Hitler. In light of this contradiction, good and evil fall along multiple axes in Soviet history, especially in the Soviet history Russians themselves have retained. These antipodes can oppose one another—good versus evil—and they can reside in one another.

For all the repressiveness, all the tyranny, and all the madness of the Soviet political economy, the Soviet Union was still a place of everyday life: a place of families and customs, and even a place that gave many of its subjects the gift of time and the unhurried, uncommercial banality of Soviet life. Over its seventy-four years, these little things gathered in a vast storehouse of Soviet sentiment and memory, a storehouse that did not disappear in 1991. In Russia and even in places that had chafed against Russian domination, people found aspects and elements of the Soviet past that they wished to hold on to.

Reagan's blanket declaration of an evil empire hid these emotions from view. For many U.S. observers, there was only one thing to say about the Soviet past: good riddance. This was their right as observers but, in saying good riddance to the Soviet Union, they adopted a schematic attitude toward the post-Soviet region. That which had broken away from the Soviet legacy was deemed good, that which remained of the

Soviet legacy was deemed bad. This scheme could make the political dynamics of the post-Soviet world unnecessarily obscure. In 2014, for example, when Ukraine descended into crisis, some of the on-the-ground disputes among Ukrainian citizens proved baffling to Americans. After a popular uprising in the capital city had toppled the Russian-leaning government, the clearest source of contention was political and geopolitical—between those who favored a new government with closer ties to Europe and those still attached to the old, Russian-leaning government. Another source was linguistic, between Ukrainian speakers and Russian speakers. But yet another was the battle over monuments—especially over statues of Lenin whose state, by 2014, had been gone for some twenty-three years.

A vague and blurry line ran across Ukraine. Lenin, of course, was peripheral to the situation, but some Ukrainians flocked to his statues, which represented the recollection of a Soviet past that had value. In the western parts of the country, the narrative was about Ukraine escaping Moscow's clutches. In the east, however, *some* counterprotests clearly remembered that it was the Red Army that had liberated Ukraine from the Germans in 1944 and 1945, having saved Ukraine from Europe, as it were. It was a matter of dueling, irreconcilable narratives. Russia fueled these disputes from the outside and intervened militarily for the sake of perpetuating them, but the disputes were not in and of themselves artificial; they were legitimately internal debates about the future of Ukrainian politics.

The foreign policy establishment in Washington, D.C., however, expressed its complete support for one side of the argument in Ukraine and was reluctant to acknowledge the other. One side appeared good, and this was the side that considered anything Soviet evil. The other side was not necessarily evil, but it was less good, in part because it appeared to be mired in the Soviet past; it had not moved on. As a result, this side was seen as the sickly flower of media—and Putin's—manipulation. By choosing sides at the beginning of this ongoing conflict and by succumbing to the Reaganite inheritance, Washington lost the chance to operate as an honest broker, to tamp down tensions on both sides, and to push them toward a mutually acceptable resolution.

AN IRONY IS that Reagan's reductive rhetoric did not impede his own foreign policy in the same way. He was more flexible than his wording implied. When he had the chance, he worked brilliantly with Gorbachev. Yet the burden of Reagan's rhetoric has grown and endured, imposing on U.S. foreign policy the unspoken attribution of goodness to the United States. This has been bad for the U.S.–Russian relationship. The underlying U.S. assumption is that Russians must accept U.S. action in Europe as a force for good. After 1945, after all, the United States brought lasting peace to Western Europe. It built up structures for the multilateral resolution of conflict, including what would become the European Union. It helped put to rest the Franco-German animosities that had resulted in two world wars. In 1989, this assumption goes, the United States managed the end of the Cold War peacefully; wisely presided over Germany's reunification; and then joined with Germany, France, and other Western European powers to extend the blessings of the Pax Americana to Central and Eastern Europe. The lynchpin of U.S. policy was granting sovereignty to small states. There would be no spheres of influence. Nobody was entitled to an empire in Europe. Lithuania had the right to choose EU and NATO membership. So, too, in theory, did Georgia and Ukraine, and this right was the cornerstone of a free and peaceful Europe.

Not every Russian would disagree with this U.S. policy toward Europe, with the benefits it has brought, and with its intellectual and strategic validity. But a great many do. There is the widely held belief in Russia, for instance, that the United States broke the promises it made about NATO at the end of the Cold War. NATO was supposed to not be expanded beyond Germany, and then it was expanded not just to Hungary, Poland, and the Czech Republic, but all the way to Estonia—a few hours' drive to Saint Petersburg. In 2008 NATO even gestured toward Georgia and Ukraine. Russians regard Western diplomacy on this point as dishonorable and the eastward drift of NATO as dangerous.

That the United States wields its power for the sake of good is anything but clear from a Russian vantage point. It is not incumbent on Russians, after all, to share the ideals of U.S. foreign policy. The United States is far away from Russia, and its culture and history are radically far away. Even though the two countries have often been allies, they have never been partners. Some degree of conflict is inevitable. Friction and government propaganda have given rise to wilder speculation: the thesis, say, that the United States has employed the CIA to sponsor a "colored revolution" in Russia; that the uprisings in Ukraine were in fact a U.S. plot; that the United States would be happy to exploit Russian resources if given the chance; or that the United States will willfully invade, destabilize, and overthrow whatever government stands in the way of its maniacal hunger for hegemony.

All of which is to say that, rational or irrational, the negative attitude toward the United States in Russia is real. It shapes Russian politics, and it orders Russian foreign policy. To anticipate Russian actions, the makers of U.S. foreign policy need to have the imagination to see themselves in the unflattering light in which they often exist in Russia. The United States may have had its reasons for expanding NATO, but it should have expected the eventual Russian response: the explosion that came in 2014. The United States also has its reasons for supporting Ukraine, but its presence there is vividly provocative to Russians—and not just to Putin and to the Kremlin.

And yet Reagan's rhetoric still hampers us today. A country that is autocratically ruled, that invaded its neighbor (Ukraine), that intervened in Syria on behalf of Bashar al-Assad, that supports antidemocratic movements worldwide, and that hacked the U.S. election of 2016 can only be evil. The temptation to think in these terms is immense, and the accusation of Russian evil haunts contemporary U.S. popular culture, media, and political discourse. But the concept of an "evil Russian empire" should be abandoned. Russia is more rational than evil; it works from its own logic and assumptions, which we are in desperate need of understanding. To reject these assumptions of evil is not to declare Russia right or unworthy of opposition. Rather, it is to make Russia legible so that a suitable response can be formulated. The United States can do more good by doing less to rid the world of evil.

Quantifying Love

Frank Pasquale

THE MOST SUCCESSFUL Internet companies, it seems, all learned the lesson of Tom Sawyer. By outsourcing labor to their users, it is as if they have cordially invited friends and neighbors to delight in painting their fence. Instagram does not need to hire photographers; users snap, post, and comment on photos, and their hashtags are a filing system, a taxonomy as meticulously curated as a filing cabinet. Instagram's parent company, Facebook, relies on all of us to keep each other amused, as does the Chinese platform Weibo. Even Google, Amazon, and Alibaba, operating far afield from social media, rely on combined consumers and producers ("prosumers") to let them know when their algorithms are helpful. They also allow customers to police the quality of products and websites so that they don't have to pay someone to do that work. Airbnb, Uber, and eBay apply similar methods, shifting the burden of quality control by having both sides in commercial transactions rate one another. We all give up small treasures—our data—to paint the fence of platform capitalists.

We may soon do the same for government. Every society depends on free labor—work that is vital but which goes unpaid. Smart governments realize that they need to strike some balance between market activity and the free labor that supports families and communities. Policymakers promote business and growth, but they also realize that if every moment were commodified, the foundations of social reproduction would wither away. Index funds may prove a better investment than children. And if you don't get credit for being civil, paying attention in class, or taking care of your aging parents, why would you?

There are standard solutions to such problems. Courts can drain the bank accounts of "deadbeat dads." Churches and civil society groups can stigmatize deviants, and the carceral state can further scare scofflaws. But these approaches take resources. The perfectly efficient neoliberal state would cut out the middleman. It would learn from Silicon Valley that you can motivate people not only to rate and rank one another, but also to positively enjoy the power and responsibility that rating (and being rated) entails.

The Chinese government is now implementing just such a system at the national level. Called the Chinese Social Credit System (SCS), it has some familiar foundations. Its early iterations (pioneered by private firms) allow users to share images of their scores with one another. As with financial credit scores used by many lenders, the system rewards people for repaying debts promptly. But the SCS does not stop with credit; it factors in court judgments, criminal records, academic dishonesty, jaywalking, moving violations, and failing to pay transit fares.

Surveillance, software, and relatively simple artificial intelligence can supply a fearsomely panoptic dossier. But this monitoring alone does not address the concern of Chinese Communist Party authorities that cornerstones of their authority are eroding. Thus the SCS will also dent your score for posting "unreliable" information or engaging in nebulously defined negative interactions online. Conversely, the system will reward volunteer activity and "filial piety"—devotion to one's parents, grandparents, and perhaps other relatives. To paraphrase Margaret Thatcher, scoring is "the method; the object is to change the heart and soul."

How can a government judge the relative value of working in the market versus visiting a lonely aunt? For the architects of the SCS, these spheres diverge: cash rules commerce, and a new currency will govern culture. That currency is reputation, a single score to express a person's social value. As China's SCS approaches its full implementation around 2020, the scoring of activities will spread, assigning points for a wider range of antisocial and social behaviors. Eventually China may make a Great Leap to Commensuration, in which every activity (or inactivity) is judged and converted to points, giving lived reality the feel of a never-ending video game.

The Chinese government claims that the SCS simply reflects the values now embodied in Chinese families, schools, and courts. But with no appeal mechanism—a basic aspect of due process in any scored society—the SCS's relentless logic of commensuration threatens to supplant, rather than supplement, the authority of families, schools, and courts. The SCS could easily end up serving as a quant-driven power grab, enabling its authors to assert authority over vast swathes of social life in a way they could never achieve via legislation. Such quantitative governance of culture is a paradox: the very effort to articulate the precise value of manners and emotions threatens to unravel them entirely, as spontaneous affections and interactions are instrumentalized into points.

WHAT THE SCS lacks in legitimacy, it makes up for in efficacy. Aspects of it are already being felt. Millions of people with low scores have been blacklisted from travel. The SCS may also eventually rely on peer scoring, a method patented (though not implemented) by Facebook in the United States. That is, if an activist criticized the government or otherwise deviated from prescribed behavior, not only would her score drop, but her family and friends' scores would also decline. This algorithmic contagion bears an uncomfortable resemblance to theories of collective punishment.

The real governance innovation in the SCS, however, is what might be called a "spiderweb" or "ripple" effect: a misdeed in one area of life can have consequences far beyond it. For example, imagine a small firm pollutes a river, and environmental regulators find out. In old governance systems, an administrator or court would assess the infraction and decide whether to impose civil or criminal penalties on the firm's owner or managers. While the outcome could be devastating for an executive, it ended there.

The new algorithmic governance of the SCS would make the pollution a problem throughout the executive's life. He might be denied the right to fly or to use the Internet—or he may need to pay more to do so. His children might be denied a place in preferred schools. Travel abroad could be rejected outright. Loans might cost more, and access to social services restricted. The SCS's stated aim is to enable the "trustworthy to roam everywhere under heaven while making it hard for the discredited to take a single step." Every "misdeed" is another step toward the internal exile of "discredit." Every merit expands the scope of one's world.

Yet this system also relies on someone defining each and every misdeed and merit. Such a system, as it expands, will eventually run into classic dilemmas of metrics. For example, every objective scoring system must embrace risk adjustment. It must give competitors some compensation for adversity beyond their control and must ensure that the lucky are not given credit merely for circumstance. A hospital in a war zone is going to have a higher mortality rate than one in Beverly Hills. So a risk adjuster tries to imagine what the average hospital copes with, and then adjusts any given hospital's score up or down based on whether it faced unusual adversity or ease.

Imagine trying to find the "average" for filial piety, one of the Chinese scoring system's cornerstones. At what point does a nagging father deserve a shortened visit from an exasperated son? Should one of three children have less obligation to spend time with her parents than a singleton? How much more does a rich person owe to his parents compared to a poor person? Each question—and countless more—will need to be answered in a quantifiable and standard way.

Without having even reached this dilemma, however, there is early anecdotal evidence that the SCS may be failing on its own terms. For example, a bank may submit false information to blackball its best customer, in order to keep that customer from seeking better terms at competing banks. To the extent that the system is a black box, there is no way for the victim to find out about the defamation.

This basic concern about data quality and integrity undermines arguments, such as the one posed by the *Financial Times*, that "Chinese AI companies, almost wholly unfettered by privacy concerns, will have a raw competitive edge when it comes to exploiting data." If guarantees of due process are limited or nonexistent, how strong can promises of data quality and integrity be? For true believers in big data, the signal of ever larger data sources will eventually drown out the noise of gamed and manipulated feeds; critics caution there is little basis to believe so.

Legal scholars in Hong Kong are already raising concerns about the SCS's accuracy and fairness. It is crucial to note, however, that if reformers focus only on legalistic concerns, their push for algorithmic accountability may miss the forest for the trees. The commensuration at the heart of the SCS is an irremediable flaw. In *Spheres of Justice* (1983), Michael Walzer defined tyranny as the domination of one mode of distribution in realms where it does not belong. It is easiest to see this domination in the realm of money and illicit commodification. If a billionaire wants to buy a beautiful handcrafted couch, few mind. However, we rightly object if the same billionaire wants to buy an election, or be first in line to receive a donated kidney, or purchase a license to travel at twice the speed limit. All those rights and privileges are supposed to be governed by some other standards: democracy, or medical necessity, or strict equality. Money becomes tyrannical when it overturns the standards of independent fields.

Algorithmic governance such as the Chinese SCS allows the government (and its private partners) to consolidate and thus dominate spheres of reputation that should be decentralized and private. It is prone to a tyrannical granularity, a spectrum of control—following Gilles Deleuze's critique of "control societies"—that is more exacting and intrusive than older forms of social order. The Chinese SCS both uses and encourages data feeds, encouraging a spiral of surveillance. One school aspires to so minutely judge citizens' lives that not even evanescent emotions are safe from scrutiny. In an experimental "intelligent classroom behavior management system" described by *Business Insider*, cameras scan classrooms every thirty seconds and record "students' facial expressions, categorizing them into happy, angry, fearful, confused, or upset . . . [as well as recording] student actions such as writing, reading, raising a hand, and sleeping at a desk." There are no limits to the regimentation a scoring system might produce. Marketed as "affective computing," these methods could easily compute optimal affect, prescribing expressions and thoughts to match them.

SADLY, the rush to monitor and measure goes well beyond the SCS. A global educational technology industry has pushed for behavioristic testing and ranking of students, schools, and teachers. The same monitoring technologies may also dominate hospitals, nursing homes, and daycare facilities. Wherever there is "soft" care to be done, untrammeled by the Taylorist impulse to measure and manage, methods like the SCS may spread. Reputational currency is a way to rebrand repression as rational nudging.

Yet if we are worried about failures in this circuit—from children raised on YouTube videos to teachers who cheat to get an edge on high-stakes exams—the answer is not to double down on performance-based ranking systems designed to shame supposed shirkers. Rather, it lies in paying good wages to teachers and caregivers, merging the spheres of society and economy that schemes such as the SCS split. Leaders must put their money where their mouths are, rather than guilt-tripping or penalizing their subjects into a zero-sum rat race for reputational currency.

Caregiving, which is notoriously underpaid labor, is especially vulnerable to neoliberalism run amok. Mike Kelley, an artist and sculptor, illustrated the discomfort society often feels when it bothers to stop and think about what it might mean to "repay" those whose work is to love and care for us. In *More Love Hours Than Can Ever Be Repaid* (1987), one of his eeriest and most affecting pieces, he assembled a wall hanging out of knitted afghans and handcrafted stuffed animals that he had purchased at thrift stores. The handicrafts exist in an uncanny netherworld. Care was poured into them, feeding affections and cathexes. They meant enough for someone to stitch them together and give them away—but not enough to be kept by the recipient.

Pasquale

To some, the patterns for these stuffed animals and shawls serve as a cliché of the culture industry, plied by *Reader's Digest* or *First* as the soft, cloth equivalent of a Betty Crocker cake. But they were channels for the expression of love. The quantification of "love hours" flattens the texture of real relationships, just as the wall hanging distorts three-dimensional stuffed animals into a flat medium. The viewer's discomfort is only alleviated by realizing that social provisioning, rather than interpersonal emotional debit accounts, can cure whatever "debts" the stuffed animals evoke. Indeed, if the state wants something done, let it pay. The real economy can then put some constraint on the quantitative governance of culture, behavior, and thought itself.

Monsters vs. Empire

Mark Bould

ON JUNE 18, 2018, President Donald Trump took everyone by surprise. In the midst of remarks about U.S. and German approaches to immigration, he was suddenly directing "the Department of Defense and Pentagon to immediately begin the process necessary to establish a space force as the sixth branch of the armed forces" and banging on about achieving "American dominance in space" and "expand[ing] our economy."

Despite Trump's seemingly abrupt change of topic, there is no actual disjuncture—indeed, there is a rather obvious continuity—between the fear of otherness and the fantasy of control, between discussing ways to restrict the movement of "undesirable" people and fantasizing about *Space Invaders*—space being, after all, the final *frontera*. There is, moreover, no contradiction between fixing borders ever more firmly in place/space and finding ways to transform the limits to capital into barriers for it to overcome. And there is no conflict between the interimperial rivalry of nation-states—both China and Russia recently demonstrated their ability to shoot down satellites—and the global Empire of transnational capital. In fact, since Ronald Reagan's neoliberal refashioning of the U.S.—and thus the global—economy in the 1980s, which transformed the world's principal source of liquidity to the world's biggest debtor, the United States has become utterly dependent on the rest of the world, including Russia and especially China, to finance its deficits. The U.S. empire needs, but does not fully control, neoliberal Empire—and the same is true of its rivals.

There has long been at the edge of the conquered world a curious interweaving of empires and monsters, the production of one depending on the production of the other. The periphery of the map always says "Here be dragons," or so we imagine. In reality, the 1510 Lenox Globe is probably the only historical map actually to bear the warning "HC SVNT DRACONES"—and even that might be less an intimation of peril than a note of where in East Asia Komodo dragons can be found. Nevertheless, cartographers have long doodled allegorical wyrms in the margins of their charts, dotted the seas with mermaids and water-spouting leviathans, and sketched strange beings in distant lands: asps, basilisks, cannibals, cynocephali, elephants, hippopotamuses, lions, scorpions, serpents, walruses—even the occasional dragon. It seems that wherever an empire's reach finds its limit, whether on Earth or in space, monsters sneak in.

JACQUES DERRIDA TALKS about two different notions of the future. There is "the future" (*le futur*), the programmed, prescribed, predictable unrolling of the present so as to perpetuate what already is, to extend the way things are. This is the future in which capital relentlessly expands and empires cling on, locking in and deepening existing relations of power. The immiseration of the peripheries. The financialization of everything. The sixth mass extinction. The carbon we have already burned, suspended in the air around us, and that which is still in the ground but which we cannot avoid burning. And then there is "the *to come*" (*l'avenir*), the unpredictable future that cannot be anticipated. "That for which we are not prepared," Derrida writes, "is heralded by species of monsters." But uncanny *arrivants* from the future are often all but impossible to distinguish from *revenants*—the ghosts which return to haunt us, the already dead that refuse to stay buried.

The classic monster returning from the past and arriving from the future is Mary Shelley's creature. *Frankenstein* (1818) begins not among the abattoirs and charnel houses from which scientist Victor Frankenstein scavenges body parts, nor in the filthy workshop of creation in which he assembles them. It starts instead with the frame tale of Robert Walton's expedition to find a navigable polar route from St. Petersburg to the Pacific, and thence to East Asia and the western coast of the Americas. He dreams noble and romantic dreams of scientific adventure, of risk and sacrifice in the pursuit of knowledge. But in reality he is bound in service to the expansion and acceleration of European power and global commerce. And it is there, near the top of the world, just as the map becomes a bare white Arctic expanse—a Georgian outer space—that Frankenstein's creature is first sighted: taken for "a savage inhabitant of some undiscovered land," he has "the shape of a man, but apparently of gigantic stature." Throughout the novel, the creature is described in this contradictory way, as both subhuman and superhuman.

On the one hand, he is as Boris Karloff portrays him in James Whale's *Frankenstein* (1931): "hideously deformed and loathsome . . . a monster, a blot upon the earth," "detestable," "horrible," "uncouth and distorted." Twice his flesh is compared to that of a mummy, a reminder that Shelley grew up during the first wave of British Egyptomania that followed Admiral Horatio Nelson's victory at the Battle of the Nile in 1798 and the French surrender of Egypt in 1801. Egyptomania really kicked off with the 1803 translation of Dominique-Vivant Denon's *Travels in Upper and Lower Egypt During the Campaign of General Bonaparte in that Country*. Replete with etchings of sublime and melancholy ruins that resonated with the Gothic mood of the times, it was a reminder that empires fall as well as rise. Egypt—hovering on the edge of integration into the circuits of European power and capital—existed in a kind of doubled time: a closing precapitalist past and an imminent capitalist future. Soon wealthy Britons were collecting artifacts and renovating rooms in Egyptian style, and, in 1812, the London Museum and Pantherion, popularly known as the Egyptian Hall, opened to the public. In this context, it would have been odd for Shelley's descriptions of her dead-but-alive creature not to evoke mummies—those uncannily preserved corpses plucked from the peripheral battlegrounds of inter-imperial rivalry and circulating in the intertwined economies of war, archaeology, popular culture, and looting.

On the other hand, Shelley's monstrous progeny anticipates Superman (though his creators never cited Shelley as an influence). The creature is "more powerful," of "superior" height, with "joints more supple"; he is "more agile," of greater "stature," better able to withstand "the extremes of heat and cold." He never leaps a tall building, but he does bound "over the crevices in the ice." And he is faster than the speeding bullet Victor fires at him, dodging it and racing away "with the swiftness of lightning." He also has a predilection for secret citadels and fortresses of solitude in alpine "ice caves" and arctic "dens."

Superman, a refugee from the technologically advanced world of Krypton, represents a form of hypermodernity. Shelley's creature, for all its necrotic pastness, likewise foreshadows futurity. When he prevails upon his maker to fashion him a female companion, he swears they will depart Europe for "the vast wilds of South America," a commons beyond empire, far "from the habitations of man." In these distant, unenclosed, and supposedly empty lands, they will live free and contented, sleeping on "a bed of leaves" and subsisting on "acorns and berries." They will tread lightly and trouble humankind no more. But Victor is unconvinced. He worries the female creature might be "ten thousand times more malignant than her mate, and delight, for its own sake, in murder and wretchedness." Or that she might lust after "the superior beauty of man" and jilt the creature, reigniting his fury at humankind. Even worse, they might breed, propagating "a race of devils . . . upon the earth" and thus making "the very existence of the species of man a condition precarious and full of terror."

Shelley's novel was shaped by the violently repressed Luddite insurgency of the 1810s. It was written while Argentine and Chilean forces were driving the Spanish from Chile. And it appeared on January 1, 1818, the same day soldiers of the British East India Company defeated their former puppet ruler Baji Rao II in the Third Anglo-Maratha War. Shelley shared the anti-colonial sympathies of her radical parents, Mary Wollstonecraft and William Godwin. But she also inherited their distrust of revolution and a preference for gradual reform—exemplified in *Frankenstein* by the politeness with which Walton's desperate yet unfailingly deferential crew mutiny against his obviously fatal plan to push on further into the perilous Arctic seas.

It is easy then to see Victor's terror of the daemonic mob that his creations might spawn as the white ruling class's terror of both the emerging industrial proletariat and the anti-colonial rebellions that together threaten to overthrow not only feudal remnants but also European imperialism and the rising bourgeoisie. If only poor Victor knew he was dreaming of a better world!

A similar contradiction can be found in H. G. Wells's *The War of the Worlds* (1897). Wells's Martian invaders reek of the past. They are vampiric monsters, their domination of an older, dying world coming to an end (an Orientalist echo, perhaps, of the devastation of China and India by British imperial and economic policies). But they are also creatures of the future. More technologically advanced than the British Empire, their massive brains, withered bodies, and hands so agile as to have become "bunches of delicate tentacles" are modelled on the future evolution of humans that Wells imagined in his 1893 essay "The Man of the Year Million—A Scientific Forecast." They are an image of what we and our world might become, and in this crucible of past and future, they crystallize the truth of the present into which they arrive.

While the novel was being serialized, British forces in the Northwest Province of India repeatedly clashed with Pashtun tribesmen, and in Southern Africa the year ended with the British colony of Natal annexing Zululand. In Wells's carnivalesque inversion, Martians from the future show the monstrousness of the world Britain had made, and make the Home Counties the battleground on which its empire is smashed.

BLOOMBERG'S RESPONSE to Trump's Space Force announcement was to commission eight designers to create a logo for this new branch of the military. David Reinfurt proposed a gold-rimmed white circle with the words "UNITED STATES SPACE FORCE" in black around the outside, so stretched as to be virtually illegible. Reinfurt describes his design as "empty at its center . . . a black hole of sorts, sucking anything that comes too close into its vortex, including even its own name." So while it is not likely to be adorning space armor or photon torpedoes any time soon, it is an apt metaphor for capital, whose logic demands the economy must constantly expand, distorting everything and leaving nothing untouched.

Trump's announcement was made just two days before the second anniversary of the world premiere of Roland Emmerich's *Independence Day: Resurgence* (2016), the belated—some might say unwanted—sequel to his 1996 box-office hit *Independence Day*. The film opens in a world transformed by alien technologies salvaged from the wrecks of the defeated invaders, and by a Pax Americana that ensures increased international cooperation to defend Earth from future threats. In the NAFTA-era original, a significant part of which is set so close to the

U.S.–Mexico border that the racist metaphors write themselves, the insectile aliens are depicted as migrant labor; when they return in the sequel, it is as an embodiment of colonial resource extraction.

The film has precisely one moment of interest. Everything is going badly. The aliens have wiped out the U.S. government. They have lured almost the entire Air Force into a lethal trap. And they are close to drilling through to Earth's core, which they intend to extract for no reason that makes any kind of sense. The ragtag remnants of the military are preparing for a fight they cannot possibly win. Which is when former president Whitmore—the Gulf War veteran responsible for defeating the aliens twenty years earlier—strides into the hangar and delivers one of those stirring patriotic speeches that everyone can hear regardless of how far away they are, even if they are wearing earmuffs. It is not as rousing as his *Independence Day* reworking of the St. Crispin's Day speech from *Henry V*, but it does contain this singular admission: "We convinced an entire generation that this is a battle that we could win. And they believed us."

Not one person in his audience—apart from David Levinson, to whom he is ostensibly speaking—looks old enough to have been born when the aliens first came, just as we are now only months away from the United States deploying its first soldier who has lived his or her entire life in a nation waging multiple simultaneous wars around the world (against an entire generation that has grown up subject to U.S. military aggression). Gilles Deleuze and Félix Guattari argue that any state which subordinates itself to "an immense war machine" and "makes war an unlimited movement with no other aim than itself" is fascist—a point appreciated by the violent satirical space opera *Starship Troopers* (1997), if not by Presidents Whitmore, Bush, Jr., Obama, or Trump. Although the aliens are defeated for a second time in *Independence Day: Resurgence*, it is still only just another battle in an ongoing conflict. The conclusion sees humankind being recruited by other alien species to lead a coalition in a war to rid the galaxy of the aliens. Everyone cheers. There is not even a pretense of reluctance to undertake this "humanitarian intervention" because sometimes it really is necessary to commit interstellar genocide in order to prevent interstellar genocide. There is just no end to the killing in sight—especially since the film's box-office performance was so poor that the intended third entry in the series was cancelled. And so we are left suspended, without resolution, without possibility of surcease.

EVEN WHEN THE ALIENS invade the entire world, the movies tend to focus on the military of an individual nation—usually the United States—defending against border incursions. At best, they imagine the global in terms of relations between nations. There is rarely any sense of Empire, of the transnational regime of finance capitalism. Its world-spanning network of information and communications technologies. Its marshalling of resources, including human labor. Its recourse, when necessary, to some nation or other's drones in the air and troops on the ground. This Empire envisions a post-historical future of peace— that is, of unperturbed accumulation—through perpetual terror and pacification. Through manufactured and managed crises, structural adjustments, capital flight, austerity, precarity, dispossession, enclosure, and debt. Through the entire repertoire of structural violence and slow violence—as well as the quicker, more spectacular kinds.

And now, it seems, through Space Force.

Vice President Mike Pence's August 9 Space Force press junket made clear that this great big bullying blustering pussy-grab for space, this effort to Make America Great Again and recover all that was lost to the perfidy of previous administrations is about just one thing: occupying the high ground. Getting out of the gravity well so as to be able to rain down shit on anyone who gets out of line. It is just a tired reboot of the old imperial fantasy of control from above. It can be traced through nineteenth-century science fiction about airborne anarchists and dirigible dictators, and through Winston Churchill's bombing of Iraqi Kurds; it can be seen in the fruity fascist overtones of the Wings Over the World global law enforcers in *Things to Come* (1936), and in the Strategic Defense Initiative first advocated by sundry SF writers and then by Ronald Reagan; and it can be seen in the murderous drone program overseen by Bush, Jr., Obama, and Trump.

And it can be seen in Joseph Kosinski's *Oblivion* (2013), which is pretty much alone among contemporary alien invasion movies in imagining beyond empires to Empire. In the film, the aliens came sixty years ago. They destroyed the Moon, and gravitational upheavals devastated the world. Then they invaded. Humans nuked them and won the most pyrrhic of victories, rendering Earth uninhabitable. The survivors abandoned the world and colonized Saturn's moon Titan. They left behind a network of monumental airborne machines to suck up the remaining water to power Titan's fusion generators (or something nonsensical like that), a drone defense network, and a maintenance worker, Jack, played by Tom Cruise. After sundry action shenanigans, Jack discovers that the deadly Scavengers intent on sabotaging the devices under his care are not remnants of the alien army but the last surviving humans, forced underground.

Jack, you see, has been played. There were no swarms of extraterrestrial warriors. Just millions of mind-wiped clones of Jack, the astronaut who first encountered the Tet—a giant, tetrahedral AI—in space. And this Jack, the one we have been following, is not the original Jack. He is just another clone deployed to accumulate for the Tet. A figure of Capital and Empire, the Tet is detached from the world, instrumentalist, without allegiance to anything human or terrestrial. It merely extracts. Wrings dry. Moves on.

There are no monsters. Just the monstrous system of Empire.

Appendix 15, Number 2. The Agent Probii Exploration

Yuri Herrera, translated by Lisa Dillman

WHEN DISCOVERY WAS MADE of this planet—the ninth one to which the iotafying machines had sent survivors, millennia ago—the first thing we did was to confirm that its inhabitants were in fact human. Aside from a few small mutations, such as growth of the outer ear and an elongation of the fingers, it was determined that they remained perfectly human. The second thing was to decipher the language in which they communicated, a feat that proved far more difficult than anticipated— not because decoding it seemed impossible, or because they spoke more than one language (a perfectly human possibility), but because what we found defied the very notion of "language."

The planet was discovered by Agent Probii, one of our best, who, despite having undertaken extraordinary research, was unable to draw the conclusions that would have saved his life. This report is based on his data.

Agent Probii's first days as undercover agent were particularly disconcerting because the city (if it can be so called) to which he arrived was lacking in stable landmarks: where one day there was a paved corner, later that night he found a wasteland; where there had been a streetlight, the following morning he found just a box of cats. Eventually he understood that this urban transience (if indeed we can employ this adjective or that noun) itself informed him of precisely what he was looking for.

It's not that the local language is unstable but that there are multiple languages, with each individual speaking only their own. Alone, at home, cooking, out for a walk, but never in dialogue. The differences between what each inhabitant speaks extend far beyond the lexical. For instance, there exist multiple ways to say "I am alive": to be stressed, alert, flowing, trembling; in addition, there are clear syntactical differences, like so:

> Stressedme.
>
> I-alert, i-alert.
>
> Meflow afterflow
>
> Sirtremblingso.

Though not every language studied exhibits agreement in gender and number (the planet's inhabitants, it would seem, are not particularly interested in numbering objects; and though there are languages recognizing two genders, others identify up to fourteen), one common characteristic is agreement in spirit. A complete sentence may introduce prefixes, infixes, or suffixes to denote the spirit in which the action is performed.

Thus, the aforementioned examples might be:

> Distressedme.
>
> Inpeace-alert, i-alert.
>
> Melliflow afterflow.
>
> Sirtremblingsobad.

And so forth.

Herrera

This tumultuous concerto of voices, which appear not to respond to one another, wrote Probii, in fact slowly engage, creating a series of intelligible utterances, asserting the desires and opinions of each person, and yet these are expressed not via a single tongue, as it were, but in a language that, though it includes words, does not depend upon them.

In order to understand it, Probii began to observe people in various phases of development. He established that, whilst babies seem to share the same tongue in the early phases of verbalization, over the course of their development this is forgotten or stops making sense. Then begins a period of introspection that lasts until the start of puberty, when, after an eternity spent in silence, adolescents watch their bodies change and quickly learn the gradations, accents, and ellipses of their physiognomy; they perfect the figuration of their flesh until arriving at what is the planet's lingua franca: copulation.

Thereafter the planet's inhabitants copulate in every imaginable way and with every participant needed in order to express themselves with precision. What is being said when one puts one hand in one place and the other in another varies quite a bit depending on what each is doing with their mouths, how many others are participating, and how slowly this is being done. The nose is vital in the communication of nuance. When words appear during the act, they are spaced out, not pragmatic objects but the accent on a sentence already being said with hips or with teeth.

This is the way relations are entered into, parties are organized, secrets revealed, recipes passed down, detailed instructions given. The planning of the city's largest bridge, for instance, required the amatory efforts of ninety-seven people at once.

Clearly it was the prospect of learning such sexual sophistication that led to Agent Probii's perdition. In the last report filed, Probii singled out one particular person with whom to enter into contact, but, incapable of understanding the multiple signs exchanged before reaching that level of communication, what he did was study the language of the person in question, learn its rudiments, and prepare a phrase that, in his judgment, would suffice for the purposes of proceeding to copulation. The phrase, in its most pragmatic translation, was something like:

"Me too please."

The precise meaning, however, is not at all important. It may be, indeed, that the person in question did not even pay attention to what Probii said. The most likely scenario, as per our subsequent reconstructions via prudent investigations with a minimum of interference, is that the very act of suddenly turning up and attempting to usurp the most intimate of possessions—this person's own, unique and inimitable tongue—was interpreted as heinous. Whether this fingered Probii as spy or devil is unknowable; the result was the same: no sooner had he demonstrated his linguistic prowess than the agent's throat was summarily slit.

It seems likely that, in the relatively near future, the inhabitants will be the ones to establish contact with us. If we've correctly interpreted the massive orgy taking place at the planet's equator for some two years now, they're in the process of imagining a space ship.

Herrera

Wajahat Ali is author of the award-winning play *The Domestic Crusaders* and a consultant for the U.S. State Department. He is a contributing op-ed writer for the *New York Times*.

Maximillian Alvarez is a dual-PhD candidate in History and Comparative Literature at the University of Michigan. He is also a columnist at the *Baffler* and hosts the podcast *Working People*.

Mark Bould teaches Film Studies at the University of the West of England, Bristol, and is author of *Science Fiction: The Routledge Film Guidebook*. He coedits the journal *Science Fiction Film and Television*.

Lisa Dillman teaches at Emory University. Her recent translations have won the 2018 Oxford-Weidenfeld Translation Award, the 2016 Best Translated Book Award, and been shortlisted for the 2018 Dublin Literary Award.

Roxanne Dunbar-Ortiz is Professor Emeritus in Ethnic Studies at California State University. She is author of *An Indigenous Peoples' History of the United States* and *Loaded: A Disarming History of the Second Amendment*.

Adom Getachew is Neubauer Family Assistant Professor of Political Science and the College at the University of Chicago. She is author of *Worldmaking after Empire: The Rise and Fall of Self-Determination*.

Yuri Herrera is Associate Professor at Tulane University and author of the novels *Kingdom Cons*, *Signs Preceding the End of the World*, and *The Transmigration of Bodies*, the translation of which (by Lisa Dillman) won the 2016 Best Translated Book Award.

Michael Kimmage is Professor of History at the Catholic University of America. He is author of *In History's Grip: Philip Roth's Newark Trilogy*.

Marisol LeBrón is Assistant Professor of Mexican American and Latina/o Studies at the University of Texas at Austin. She is author of *Policing Life and Death: Race, Violence, and Resistance in Puerto Rico* and a cocreator of the Puerto Rico Syllabus, a digital resource for understanding the Puerto Rican debt crisis.

Pankaj Mishra is author of *Age of Anger: A History of the Present* and recipient of the Windham–Campbell Literature Prize for nonfiction.

Jeanne Morefield is Professor of Politics at Whitman College and will soon join the Department of Political Science and International Studies at The University of Birmingham. She is the author of *Empires Without Imperialism: Anglo-American Decline and the Politics of Deflection* and *Covenants Without Swords: Idealist Liberalism and the Spirit of Empire.*

Frank Pasquale is Professor of Law at the University of Maryland and the author of *The Black Box Society: The Secret Algorithms that Control Money and Information.*

Arundhati Roy is the author of *The Ministry of Utmost Happiness* and won the Man Booker Prize for *The God of Small Things.*

Stuart Schrader is Lecturer in Sociology at Johns Hopkins University and completing a book for University of California Press on the domestic effects of U.S. counterinsurgency efforts overseas during the Cold War.

Avni Sejpal is a graduate student in English at Villanova University. She was previously an associate editor at *Boston Review.*

Nikhil Pal Singh is Professor of Social and Cultural Analysis and History at New York University and Faculty Director of the NYU Prison Education Program. His most recent book is *Race and America's Long War.*